T0295764

The Field Guide to Achieving HR Excellence through Six Sigma

The Field Guide to Achieving HR Excellence through Six Sigma

Daniel Bloom

CRC Press
Taylor & Francis Group
Boca Raton   London   New York

CRC Press is an imprint of the
Taylor & Francis Group, an **informa** business

A PRODUCTIVITY PRESS BOOK

CRC Press
Taylor & Francis Group
6000 Broken Sound Parkway NW, Suite 300
Boca Raton, FL 33487-2742

© 2016 by Daniel Bloom
CRC Press is an imprint of Taylor & Francis Group, an Informa business

No claim to original U.S. Government works

Printed by CPI on sustainably sourced paper
Version Date: 20160105

International Standard Book Number-13: 978-1-4987-1567-6 (Paperback)

Library of Congress Cataloging-in-Publication Data

Names: Bloom, Daniel, author.
Title: The field guide to achieving HR excellence through six sigma / Daniel Bloom.
Description: Boca Raton, FL : CRC Press, 2015. | Includes bibliographical references and index.
Identifiers: LCCN 2015045187 | ISBN 9781498715676 (alk. paper)
Subjects: LCSH: Personnel management. | Six sigma (Quality control standard) | Organizational effectiveness.
Classification: LCC HF5549 .B7253 2015 | DDC 658.3/01--dc23
LC record available at http://lccn.loc.gov/2015045187

Visit the Taylor & Francis Web site at
http://www.taylorandfrancis.com

and the CRC Press Web site at
http://www.crcpress.com

Contents

List of Figures

List of Exercises

Preface

On August 28, 1963, Dr. Martin Luther King delivered his iconic "I have a Dream Speech." Like Dr. King, I, too, have a dream or more correctly a vision. While I am not referring to my four-year-old son as Dr. King did, I am referring to our global workplace. Let Me paraphrase Dr. King's speech and relate my vision or dream to you, the reader.

I have a goal in my professional life to deliver a message. It is a message that will transform our business world to greater heights. Today, this installment will lay out this vision for you, the reader.

If we go back to the time of the Emancipation Proclamation, we were deeply involved in the agricultural age. This was a period when the family ran the farm and each individual had an integral part in the success of the farm. As we moved to the industrial age, we lost that human capital asset focus.

In a sense, we have come to this point in our business development to cash a check. Starting with the Quaker business model, business laid out a promise to the organization that management would take care of its most valuable tool in its arsenal to compete in the global marketplace—the human capital assets that are now nonowned, leased corporate assets. This promise stated that all programs initiated by the organization would be centered on a guarantee of being a valued part of the organization. As we look at many organizations today, it increasingly obvious that American business has defaulted on this promise. The focus moved from considering the human capital asset as such to being an expense item that affected the corporate bottom line.

But we refuse to believe that the promise is bankrupt. We refuse to believe that there is no room for organizations to change in the global workplace. So we are writing this book to show the way to reclaim that promise. It would be fatal for business to ignore this message. This means, as Dr. Deming suggested, we need to move to a new philosophy in which management learns its responsibilities and takes on leadership for change.

This change establishes some clear indicators of success.

■ First, we need to rid the organization of the words "It is not my job." The move to a quality focus is based on the practice of spreading quality throughout the organization so that it becomes everyone's job.
■ Second, we must allow the rank and file the authority to make changes to the process if what they see is causing the organization to not meet the needs of the customer.
■ Third, we must recognize the worth of everyone involved in the organizational processes.

This journey of change is not one we can walk alone. And as we embark on this journey, we must make the pledge that we shall always march ahead. It means we must remove from organizational vernacular the objections to moving forward. It means that it must be all hands on deck in this new philosophy. It must become the corporate mantra that quality is the primary focus of the way we do business. Everyone must learn the keys to reaching that goal and then spreading the message to the organization and our customers. The organization must realize that we cannot turn back once we begin this journey.

I am not unmindful that some of you have read this preface with great trials and tribulations. You have come from a world that is embedded in a tradition that says this is not the way we do things here. Some of you have been confronted by organizations very much averse to doing things differently. You have been the victims of command and control organizational structures. Know and understand it has to change.

I have a dream that one day our businesses will understand what quality means and practice it every day.

I have a dream that one day our organizations will understand that the quick buck is not the solution to organizational sustainability.

I have a dream that one day all our organizations will learn the language of business and understand that process metrics are there to make us better, not hold us back.

I have a dream that one day management and our human capital assets will all be on the same page as far as producing the products and services we are known for, without error.

This is my hope and this is the faith that I go forward with—that there are better days coming: days rooted in doing things right the first and every time, and rooted in believing that we all have a responsibility to meet the voice of the customer in every interaction we have with them.

Join me on this exciting and dynamic journey. Join me in this effort to vastly improve the focus of our organizations within the global workplace. Together we can create a different business world in which we are all on the same page.

This sequel to *Achieving HR Excellence through Six Sigma* is the path to my vision.

Eighteen years ago, Dave Ulrich and the team at the RBL Group took us on a journey with the publication of *Human Resource Champions.*[*] In his book, Ulrich suggested that there were four roles for human resource professionals—strategic partner, administrative expert, employee champion, and the change agent. In order to transform our organizations to this new business model, it required a transformational journey that was riddled with both obstacles and challenges. This model required management and the organization as a whole to completely change the way they see not only the organization but also the way in which it operates. This transformational journey required a change in the way organizations functioned along with a new normal in the form of a changed corporate culture.

Recently, the Society for Human Resource Management (SHRM) has undertaken a drive to introduce the SHRM Competency Model,[†] which at its core involves much of what Ulrich and others have been calling for. If you dissect the competency model, while not in specific terms, it makes

---

[*] Ulrich, Dave. *Human Resources Champions*. Boston, MA: Harvard Business School Press, 1997.
[†] Society for Human Resource Management. *SHRM Competency Model*. http://www.shrm.org /hrcompetencies/pages/default.aspx

references to competencies that are included in the Theory of Constraints–Lean–Six Sigma (TLS) Continuum methodology outlined in the prior work. The problem with these discussions has been that while the concepts are needed and at this point in time are almost a requirement for the sustainability of our organizations, there has been no clear concept or road map on how to accomplish this transformation.

This journey of transformation involves a difficult and challenging effort. I know because I have taken the journey. In 2001, I read a book, which turned my whole outlook toward business in a total new direction. That book was *The Goal*,[*] by Dr. Eliyahu Goldratt. This phenomenal book led me, with the assistance of Dr. James Holt at the University of Washington–Vancouver, to write an article for *Mobility Magazine* titled "Driving the Relocation 500"[†] in which I utilized the theory of constraints to reduce by half the timeline required to return an employee to full productivity following the relocation of the employee and his or her family.

In 2008, I made the decision to return to higher education to expand my knowledge of continuous process improvement by undergoing the grueling process of earning certification as a Six Sigma Black Belt. Combined with my over 30 years of human resource experience, it became a natural progression to combine the two disciplines. It enabled me to see organizations in a whole new light.

The quest for this new culture was the impetus in 2013, through Productivity Press, for my writing the book titled *Achieving HR Excellence through Six Sigma*,[‡] which was taken out of the 2-day seminar we developed in 2009. The seminar provided a road map for human resource professionals from which the attendees could learn the process of introducing this change to their organizations. You will see in Chapter 7 how one of the seminar attendees made some dramatic improvements in the human resources (HR) function.

I have taken the transformational journey described above to the degree that I believe I have reached the goal of being of able to look at organizations to discern the concepts of what is holding them back from becoming truly productive in their industries. The journey has at its basis a new perspective as the anticipated outcome of this sequel to the original

---

[*] Goldratt, Eliyahu. *The Goal*. North River Press. Croton-on-the-Hudson, NY: Northern River Press, 1984.

[†] Bloom, Daniel. Driving the Relocation 500. *Mobility* magazine, October, 2001.

[‡] *Achieving HR Excellence through Six Sigma* released by Productivity Press on August 13, 2013. See the Productivity Press website at http://www.crcpress.com/product/isbn/9781466586468.

volume. You, the reader, can take the same journey with the understanding that it is unique at best.

Just to ensure that we are on the same page as we begin the journey, think back to the last family vacation you planned. What steps did you take in planning that last trip? If you are the typical family, you looked at the calendar and decided when you planned on leaving. You also planned out when your expected return was.

With the beginning and ending dates in place, you began to determine how you were going to get there and where you were going to stay. This is a very consistent scenario for most planned family vacations.

The intent of *The Field Guide to Achieving HR Excellence through Six Sigma* is to take you on a different kind of journey. This journey of continuous process improvement meets none of the criteria I discussed above. I can state unequivocally when we are leaving. We are leaving on this journey when the organization realizes that they have an urgent problem that must be addressed. They also understand that the status quo will not serve the issues required to solve the problems. That is the sole thing I can relate to you. We do not know how we are going to get there. We don't even know where we are going or how long we are staying. We don't even know what we are returning to.

This journey has two primary key performance indicators (KPIs) that form the basis of this book. First, we will never return to where we began. We can't go back to that point in time because it no longer exists. The old normal has gone the way of the dinosaurs. Management has transformed into authentic leaders and away from being managers. We do not and cannot serve our human capital assets and our stakeholders from a command and control perspective. We have been forced into looking at our organizations and workplaces with the view of being a coach, teacher, and mentor. Human capital assets are now true partners in the success of the organization. Our roles have changed and so has the culture of the organization. The organization is "forced" into recognizing the worth of the entire human capital asset components within the operation setting. The direct result is that we now run our organizations from collaborative teams, which cross all boundaries in the organization.

Second, we do not have an ending point because we are entering into a journey where the final destination is under constant reconstruction. This journey can be difficult but it also can be enlightening as the result is a new level of productivity on the part of the total organization. I understand the trials and tribulations of this journey because I have been there.

It is my intent, therefore, to take you on this journey through the pages of the book you have in your hands. Consider that the end result of our time together will be the basis for a new process of solving your organizational problems. Consider the end result being the identification of changes that will make the organization more efficient and sustainable in the long run. I will equip you with the knowledge to take your organization into the future.

A word of caution is required at this point. If the reason you are looking at the former work flow and the present one is to discover a method to reduce headcount, then you should stop here and now. Thank you for the visit but this is not the place for you. Only if you are on the verge of closing the business should headcount reduction be the primary reason for you taking this journey.

Returning to our journey, what I discovered was that the implementation of the TLS Continuum methodology was the journey. It requires us to continue with an open mind, as this is like nothing you have ever ventured before. It requires you to have the ability to challenge everything you do. This journey will be difficult for some, as it requires that we break long-established rules. It requires that you forget what is considered normal for your organization. It requires you to change the corporate culture from that which is comfortable. It requires us to look at things differently. *Achieving HR Excellence through Six Sigma* provided us with the road map to understand the new direction. It clearly identified where we started from with the work of Dr. W. Edwards Deming. It gave us a look at how some organizations have laid the path for you by successfully implementing these tools within their organizations. However, not every organization is a DuPont or a Ceridian. So the question becomes, do we understand that we need to make these changes in order to be competitive in the global workplace? Do we understand how the organization goes about making the changes called for?

The Field Guide to Achieving HR Excellence through Six Sigma will answer those questions. It is designed to take you step by step along this journey. Further, it will provide you with focused results-oriented solutions to empower you to change your organization. It will provide you with a clear picture of where your organization is failing to meet the voice of the customer.

Let's begin the journey. Fasten your seat belts because it is going to be a rocky ride. We can't change the culture of the organization without experiencing some turbulence from those who are resistant to change. I get that not everyone is comfortable with changing the status quo, but we are left with no other choice. The reason for this is, like any evidence-based effort, we can't tell you what the evidence will show until we are finished. In addition, the continuous process improvement effort, by its very nature, is a constant exercise within your organization. Once you resolve one issue another pops its head up and likewise needs to be resolved.

Unlike its predecessor, this volume is a field guide designed to provide you with step-by-step processes to take you on your own journey to an organization that is strategic, innovative, and aligned with the organization mission. It will lay out how we get from identifying the problem to the initial resolution of the issue.

Earlier, I discussed brief descriptions of the steps we take to plan out a family trip. To make this journey clear, I will use the same steps. This field guide consists of seven chapters; each one is a counterpart to the steps outlined below. Each chapter will also include exercises for you to plan your own journey. We will keep that journey theme as we progress to show what we have achieved.

Chapter 1. Creating a Center of Excellence—The subtheme of this field guide is *How to Create an HR Center of Excellence*. In order to lay the groundwork for that task, we will return to the first chapter of the prior work and expand our definition of HR Excellence. I will return to the view of the anonymous definition and look at how that impacts your career. The definition will provide us the understanding as to what a center of excellence is.

Chapter 2. Preboarding: Seeing the Problem—Every journey begins with a road map of how we intend to reach the destination. In the case of the continuous process improvement effort, it begins with identifying the problem—seeing where we are not meeting the voice of the customer. The chapter lays out a step-by-step method to recognize the problems you face.

Chapter 3. Flight to Excellence—The second stage is to feel the problem. We feel the problem by gaining an understanding of how the problem is affecting the organization. I will show you how to enter the second stage of the process—measuring the impact of the results of your problem definition.

Chapter 4. Layover—Obstacles to Improvement—Chapter 4 considers the reasoning behind our belief that this journey is difficult at best. We, as humans, tend to resist change. But this journey mandates a change to a new normal. This chapter looks at the bull in the china shop and considers the arguments that may be posed in objection to the change you are proposing.

Chapter 5. Where Oh Where Is the End of This Journey?—This chapter covers the final two stages of the DMAIC (define–measure–analyze–improve–control) process, looking at the steps to improve the process and create the standard of work. It also discusses the future of your improvement efforts.

Chapter 6. This Is Where I Get Off—There is only so much I can do to guide you along this fantastic journey. There is a point at which you have to take responsibility for your own future. There is a point when you have to take control of the process. In this chapter, I provide guidelines on where to go next based on the concepts discussed in Chapter 9 of the original book.

Chapter 7. Case Studies—Unlike the original book, these case studies are different in nature. In the original work, I presented a number of case studies of organizations that had successfully utilized the Six Sigma methodology to improve and correct HR issues. As is typical of most case studies, they were written in narrative form, creating a story behind the project. I wanted to try something different in this field guide. As a result, these case studies are presented in a different format. The only narrative is in the form of two short paragraphs. The first contains a brief description of the organization involved. The second is a description of the problem being presented.

Following these two paragraphs, the corporations have generously permitted us to show the exact project documents used by the organization. These include the project charter, and any other documents associated with the project.

If you are reading this book because you read *Achieving HR Excellence* and wanted more information, we welcome you back. If you are reading this book because the idea sounded interesting, join the ride. It will be fun.

So fasten your seat belts and let's begin this unique journey.

Acknowledgments

The Field Guide to Achieving HR Excellence through Six Sigma is my third effort at writing a book. After writing three books, one lesson that I have learned is that these endeavors do not operate in a vacuum. The ability to get my message to the reader is dependent on a wide range of people with a wide range of talents. Each of them, in their own way, contributes to the success of the project.

First of all, I must thank the people at Taylor & Francis and Productivity Press for their willingness to give a relatively unknown writer a chance on the book on which this book is based and then again to be willing to publish the sequel. I especially need to thank executive editor Michael Sinocchi and project coordinator Jessica Vakili for their guidance through the process. Once again, as I did on *Achieving HR Excellence through Six Sigma*, it was a pleasure to work with project editor Iris Fahrer on the sequel to that work.

Peter Pande in his works in the Six Sigma arena stresses that there is no single Six Sigma way. So while the road map presented in this book is my own thoughts about the way to guide human resource professionals on this journey, I have greatly appreciated having this project reviewed by peers in the field. My thanks go out to Bob Sproull, author of the *Ultimate Improvement Cycle* and *Epiphanized* to ensure I got the TOC component correct and to William Mazurek who, since my Six Sigma training, has been my sensei and friend and offered continued support in my efforts. I also would like to thank Steven Bonacorsi who helped with the material regarding the Ishikawa diagram and helped fill in some of the holes as I proceeded through the material in this book. Finally to my neighbor, Don Easterday, an engineer with the local operations of a Fortune 1000 organization, for his willingness to review this journey for its accuracies and implications for organizations.

The question of a good definition for transformational leader is elusive at best. I appreciate the assistance of Bob Sproull, Loren Murfield, Larry Williams, and Kent Linder for their input on this critical part of *The Field Guide*. I am not sure we reached that golden consensus on the meaning of a transformational leader but their input has been greatly appreciated. This is in part because everyone has his or her own individual view about what a transformational leader is or should be.

Each of us has our own unique learning styles, based on how we intake information. Some of us are more visual than others. Some are more verbal than others. Some are more physical in nature. I have tried in these pages to present the opportunity for you, the reader, to learn the implementation process based on your individual learning style. So for those who are more visual, I have to thank the management and HR staff at Sparton Electronics. Their HR manager, Lorri Kindberg, participated in my 2-day seminar from which this material is based and the second case study in Chapter 7 is the result of her final project for that seminar. I also extend my thanks for their participation in compiling projects that would show visual learners how to implement a project along with the accompanying documents to show you a project in action. As always, William Mazurek, my black belt instructor, has been there when I needed help. In this case, he contributed three additional projects for the case study chapter.

I am equally appreciative of my peers within the HR profession who have endorsed the context that I presented here is the correct context given the rapidly changing organizational playing field: Tresha Moreland, vice president of Human Resources for the Dameron Hospital Association in Stockton, California; Nicole Ochenduski, HR manager with Church & Dwight Company Ohio facility; Bob Sproull, the author of *Epiphanized*; Gary DePaul, organizational development consultant; and Christina Gasperino, formerly an HR manager with KForce and currently the director of Employee Relations and Services with Wellcare Health Plans.

Author

Daniel T. Bloom, SPHR, SSBB, SCRP, is the founder and chief executive officer of Daniel Bloom & Associates, Inc. Founded in 1980, DBAI is a Largo, Florida–based human capital consulting firm dedicated to helping clients to create strategic, innovative, and aligned organizations. His clients represent a wide range of organizations from small organizations to members of the Fortune 1000.

Daniel is a well-respected author, speaker, and human resource strategist, who, during his career, has worked in a wide variety of industries. He has been an educator, a contingency executive recruiter, a member of a Fortune 1000 divisional HR staff, and the corporate relocation director for several real estate firms in the Tampa Bay area. He has been an active member of the HR social media scene since 2006 with contributions to Best Thinking.com, Blogger, WordPress, Human Capital League, and recruiting blogs. He also serves as a moderator of the Lean Six Sigma HR group and a manager of the Brandergy groups on LinkedIn. He is also a frequent contributor to the HR site Hirecentrix.

He has published two books—*Just Get Me There* in 2005 which is the documented history of the corporate relocation industry and *Achieving HR Excellence through Six Sigma* published in 2013. He has also written more than 40 articles on various HR issues that have appeared both in print and online.

Daniel is a member of the Suncoast HR Association, Worldwide ERC, National Speakers Association, the MBA Coaching Program at the University of Tampa, and the Engineering Technology and Building Arts Advisory Board of St. Petersburg College.

He earned a bachelor's of arts degree in education from Parsons College and his Six Sigma Black Belt from the Engineering and Technology Program at St. Petersburg College. He holds certification as a Senior Professional in human resources, a Six Sigma Black Belt, and a Senior Certified Relocation Professional.

List of Abbreviations

DHR	device history record
DMAIC	define–measure–analyze–improve–control
DOP	department operating procedures
DPMO	defects per million opportunities
FTE	Full time equivalent employee
HIPOS	high potential, high performing
HR	human resources
KPI	key performance indicators
MSA	measurement system analysis
NCR	nonconformance report
SEO	search engine optimization
SHRM	Society for Human Resource Management
SMEs	subject matter experts
SMEs	small to medium enterprises
TLS	Theory of Constraints–Lean–Six Sigma

Chapter 1

Creating a Center of Excellence

Achieving HR excellence is the result of CARING more about your organization than others think wise; RISKING more than others think safe to change the corporate culture; DREAMING more than others think practical about the potential of your organization; EXPECTING more than others find possible from your human capital assets

The subtheme of this *Field Guide to Achieving HR Excellence through Six Sigma* is *The Creation of a Human Resource (HR) Center of Excellence*. The Six Sigma problem-solving methodology requires that we must begin by defining the problem. For us the first step begins with defining the term "Center of Excellence." Part of the difficulty here is that there is apparently no general consensus as to what the term means. There is some agreement that Centers of Excellence involve four traits.

First, the organization creating the Center takes the necessary steps to improve its own expertise. This expertise improvement goes beyond the HR department. It means as HR professionals we must understand the whole organization. We must understand the process flow from the front door to the rear door and all the steps along the way. The intended output is for the HR department to be recognized as the primary source of information on a wide range of human capital management issues. We achieve this by demonstrating to the various parts of the organization that we understand the organizational alignment and the strategic direction.

Second, the Center of Excellence provides the development of the resources necessary for HR and others to reach that expertise level. These resources may include data, information, training, and other vehicles to lay the groundwork necessary to assist the organizational assets to learn what they must achieve to reach the levels they are seeking. HRs must become the go-to person for how the changes we propose will affect the talent management of the organization.

Third, the Center of Excellence effort requires a change in the corporate culture. The move to a Center of Excellence is not a fad thing. The move is not a here in the moment thing where we do it now but give us a week and we will have gone on to something different. It is a permanent fixture within your organization. It is an aspect of the community we call a corporation that is ever present in how we operate. It is not a department; it is an ongoing process.

Fourth and finally, the expectation is that the Centers of Excellence will share their newfound expertise throughout the organization. As you obtain the status of experts it becomes your responsibility to spread the message to the other functions that have not found the way as of yet. As we achieve new milestones in our improvement effort we have a duty to show others how they can achieve the same or better results. It is your responsibility—no make that *duty*—to further share the vision we discussed earlier with your organization.

Beyond the discussion of the components above, there is no definitive definition for a Center of Excellence. The Internet does not help us gain a further understanding to the term either. If you Google "Centres of Excellence," the search engine returns 50,900,000 specific entries. If you turn around and change the spelling of "Centres" to the more American version and spell it "Centers" you get back 53,100,000 entries. To further confuse the issue, the vast majority of the entries are for organizations that have Centers or Centers of Excellence rather than looking at the specific characteristics of the term. We can't create what we don't understand. It is therefore critical that we determine a definition for the end result of what this book is set out to accomplish. It is critical that we believe both in the established definition of Centers of Excellence and the impact of them in the workplace.

In this chapter, I discussed several definitions of what we mean by the term "HR excellence." My primary emphasis was on an anonymous quote reportedly on the wall at the United States Military Academy at West Point. Based on this definition, I proposed the ultimate definition of "HR excellence." That definition can be found by looking at the quotation at the beginning of this chapter. To help us with the creation process, I want to take some time and further explore this definition. That path is shown in the following.

CARING More about Your Organization than Others Think Wise

The first component of the definition is that *you need to care more about your organization than others think wise*. There is much discussion these days about the level of employee engagement in our organizations. What is common in many organizations is that we tuck away our functions into these convenient pigeonholes called silos. These silos become this grand world within a world with formidable borders that are not supposed to be breached. Their very existence is supported and challenged by internal politics and turf wars.

We see these silos in action when we approach either an internal colleague or an external customer and the response to our request is "that is not my job." We tend to fail to look at the entire global picture and our roles in it. The common reaction is that if you dare to go outside these narrow confines you are risking your career or, even more ominous, you are risking the sustainability of the organization. The problem is that this becomes a continuous cycle. Every time we go to someone and we are told the solution is "not my job," it further ingrains in the organization the belief that this is just the way we do things here. There is no room for discussion or a different way of doing things.

Look around your organization: What do you see? I would hazard the guess that in many organizations you consistently hear the response "It is not my job." The Center of Excellence requires a deeper sense of belonging. The West Point definition suggests that excellence is a set of behaviors or actions that manifest themselves in how we are perceived by the organization and the marketplace. It suggests that in order to achieve a state of excellence, we are required to change from the path of least resistance to more involvement in the outcomes. The changes are required both on an individual basis and on an organizational level. It further suggests that in order to achieve a state of excellence you have to be an active participant in that change process. In order to create this culture change we need to expand the view beyond the silo mentality. We need to look at the organization from a macro view.

Exercise 1.1 What Does Your Job Description Tell You about Your Role in the Organization?

The purpose of the job description is to detail what key performance indicators are required to effectively perform the duties and responsibilities of the position.

_____

_____

_____

_____

According to Robert L. Mathis, in his *Human Resource Management,*[*] a job description along with the job specifications define what the organization expects from the position and what that position contributes to the total organizational structure. We begin the process of uncovering the role we play by examining our individual roles within the organization. A properly written job description should detail the extent to which you have the ability to influence what goes on within the HR function. A properly written job description should detail the extent to which you have the ability to influence what goes on within the entire organization. Does the wording of your job description indicate the extent of your ability to be able to seek out and try to remove those activities that are hindering the HR department and the organization? However, the job description is only the beginning stage of our examination of this issue.

Exercise 1.2 Describe the Extent You Are Involved in the HR Function of Your Organization

Are you involved in a mini silo within HR or are you part of a bigger picture?

_____

_____

_____

_____

---

[*] Mathis, Robert L. *Human Resource Management.* 12th Edition. Mason, OH: Thomson/Southwest, 2008. p. 186.

Consider your position. Based on your review of your position, what would your response be to the following questions?

■ Are you involved in routine tasks that are done almost by rote or are your tasks involved in the total operation of the department?
■ Does your job description allow for you to use critical-thinking skills in the performance of those duties?
■ If push came to shove could you do your peer's job if they were not present?

Creating a Center of Excellence requires us to have involvement in cross-functional teams whose purpose is to make the operations of the organization run more efficiently throughout the organization, not just in HR. Therefore, in order to achieve this we must be involved in the total effort.

Exercise 1.3   Describe the Extent You Are Involved in the Organizational Improvement Process

If we accept the premise that the key here is the existence of cross-functional teams, how involved are you in this effort?

_____

_____

_____

_____

What is the reach of your involvement? Can you make suggestions for process changes that are reasonably considered or are they counted against you for rocking the boat? I stated earlier that you must get out of your silo and be part of the total organization. As a result, we must be part of the entire improvement effort. This means that HR must be involved not only in the HR improvement efforts but also those taking place in marketing, sales, finance, purchasing, communications, and legal. If there is an improvement effort going on within the organization anywhere HR must be involved. The reasoning for this is that whenever your improvement process involves the human capital assets of the organization, HR as the talent gatekeeper has a vital role in that effort.

RISKING More than Others Think Safe to Change the Corporate Culture

I totally get it that the easy way out is to play it safe. We are forever hearing of professionals being told "don't rock the boat." The status quo is fine. If there is a chance that it will fail, don't do it. If it might affect this cushy job you got, don't do it. But understand this: change is inevitable. The sustainability of your profession and your organization demands that you take risks. Along with change comes risk. So take some.

Exercise 1.4 If an Individual Employee Takes the Initiative to Make a Change to a Process for the Better, How Does Management Respond?

    Change = Risk = Improvement

_____

_____

_____

_____

We can't change the organization without undergoing some level of risk. We risk that we might fail in the attempt to change the organization. We risk that we might have the wrong human capital assets involved in the new process. We risk that the human capital assets may not accept the change. We risk that management might put up obstacles to achieve the goals we have set. We risk that our customers may not understand why we are changing the operating procedures. We are left with no option but to take the risk when we proceed. On the other side of the coin, we are at risk when we decide to keep the status quo. We would not be suggesting the change initiative unless we had to for the sustainability of the organization. The Six Sigma methodology brings about a change in the corporate culture. We can't take this journey without changing the corporate culture. The very nature of that change is risk-abound.

    The problem comes about when the organization does not walk the walk and talk the talk. When the organization issues empty dialogue to the FTEs regarding their belief in experimentation, we fail to recognize the risk involved. We have all seen these situations. The corporation makes some changes to a process and then a month later it changes again. The talk that we present to the marketplace is that we are supportive of our human capital assets thinking out of the box. We encourage them to make changes where they see the need but if the change fails we then penalize them for trying. We count it against them in their annual performance review. We count it against them in their annual raises. Contrary to the advice of Dr. W. Edwards Deming, we count it against them when they don't make quota.

The result of the dichotomy is that the human capital assets become accustomed to the policy that the organization says we are supportive of change but don't try. Taking the risk is not beneficial to the employees or to the HR function. The status quo becomes the ingrained method of operation.

The purpose of Exercise 1.4 is for you to assess how your organization responds to the initiatives of your employees. When it comes to risk issues do you walk the walk and talk the talk? Suggest a change to your organization and what does your management say? Do they tell you let's go with it as in the GE Workout or the Change Acceleration Process?* Do they tell you to let it go because that is just not the way we do things here?

DREAMING More than Others Think Practical about the Potential of Your Organization

Human nature tends to limit what we see in our environment that surrounds us not only as individuals but also as organizations. We conceive this idea in our minds as to what is possible. The problem is in most cases it narrows the potential of the organization. Our schools no longer teach critical-thinking skills. Based on our cultural upbringing, we look at the world around us with rose-colored glasses which only see a partial view of the world.

Exercise 1.5   Has This Happened to You?

You discover an easy way to enhance the organization. You prepare the arguments as to why and how this can be introduced to your organization and management says no.

_____

_____

_____

_____

Management has the tendency to look at the world with the same rose-colored glasses. Changes to an organization are filtered through the existing corporate culture that may very well be centered on false reasoning.

---

* For a more in-depth understanding of the GE Workout process, I suggest that readers take a look at David Ulrich's book on the topic, *GE Workout.* New York, NY: McGraw-Hill, 2002.

At some time in the past, someone attended some conference and heard an idea that sounded good to them. They returned to the organization and implemented the idea years ago. The problem is that this idea may very well not be good strategy today. However, since it was implemented years ago, it remains ingrained within the organization and not subject to change. This journey we are on will very well mandate just that change.

EXPECTING More than Others Find Possible from Your Human Capital Assets

The final part of the HR excellence definition is a look at the organizational potential. Numerous studies have shown that we tend to make decisions as to someone's potential within the first 4–6 seconds after we meet them. We develop these stereotypes and they cloud our views going forward. Our look at stereotypes says John Doe is not capable of performing a particular task based solely on our view of that person.

Exercise 1.6 Employee Stereotypes

What is your organizational attitude toward the capabilities of the human capital assets in your organization?

_____

_____

_____

_____

If you are like most managers, your tendencies are to believe that your FTEs are fixed in space as to what they are capable of. The capabilities of your human capital assets can be defined in several fashions.

- First, there are the innate skills they bring with them. These skills come from their education, training, and upbringing. They are skills that are representative of the basic abilities we bring to the table.
- Second, there are skills that the human capital assets learn through the training programs that your organization provides. Primarily centered on skills that are needed to meet the key performance indicators of the positions.

Two very different sides of a spectrum influence the skill abilities of our FTEs. One side of the spectrum is represented by the will of the FTEs to learn those skills. As organizations resist change so do our employees. As much as we may try we can't always get every FTE to come to the feeding trough. No matter what we do they will not learn the new skills required. In these cases, the best course of action is to coach the individual out of your organization.

At the other side of the spectrum are the FTEs who are open to undergoing training to educate them in the required skills. With these employees, it is necessary that we recognize that once we have educated them on the new key performance indicators (KPIs), we may very well have to provide additional coaching to get them up to speed. The final aspect of the Center of Excellence definition is to bring the skills to others within the organization.

The bottom line of the process to create the Center of Excellence in HR is to change the way we think and feel about our organizations. We need to strive to become the organizational experts in regard to the impact of the human capital assets within the organization. This includes the developing and maintaining of the resources needed to help the organization also become the experts in what they do. When we accomplish this we create a permanent change in the culture. The Center of Excellence becomes a permanent part of the organization.

In the succeeding chapters, I will lead you through this process in a clearly defined step-by-step road map. Once you have followed the road map, you will create the critical Center of Excellence within the HR function.

Let's continue the journey.

Chapter 2

Preboarding: Seeing the Problem

> Good afternoon passengers. This is the pre-boarding
> announcement for TLS Continuum flight 2014 to Destination
> Unknown. We are now inviting those passengers who contribute to
> our sustainability to begin boarding at this time. Please have your
> boarding pass and identification ready. Regular boarding will begin
> in approximately ten minutes time. Thank you.[*]

Seeing the problem is the beginning of our journey. It entails identifying
several components of a successful journey as described earlier. We need to
identify who is going on this journey, how do we plan on getting there, and
why we are going on the journey.

Prior to beginning this part of the journey, I need to step back from our
journey and take a moment to try and relay my take on an ongoing argument
that is taking place in Corporate America. This is the endless debate
regarding whether we are talking about shareholders versus stakeholders.

While the two terms are interrelated, they are in reality two different groups
of organizational constituents. We begin with the concept of shareholders.
The theory behind the shareholder assumes that the reason your organization
exists is to earn a profit.[†] That is what the basis is for chief executive officer

---

[*] The dialogue is taken from a sample captain's speech found on the website http://airodyssey.net
/reference/inflight/
[†] http://www.corplaw.ie/blog/bid/317212/Shareholder-Stakeholder-Theories-Of-Corporate-
Governance

(CEO) evaluations. This is what justifies the CEO's job. That is what the goal is for the efforts of the chief financial officer (CFO). This is what the board of directors uses to determine the strategy for the organization. The fallacy with this narrow view is that we are referring to only those individuals and entities that have a vested *financial* interest in your organization. Typically, this means they have in their possession shares of stock in your organization.

I guarantee that if you start using the term "stakeholders" around the office someone will challenge you by stating directly or indirectly, "Listen stupid, we are only concerned with the shareholders." The argument suggests that unless you have a physical financial investment in the organization your thoughts, needs, and wants are of no consequence. Therefore, everything we do or everything we say is designed to answer to the shareholders about whether we are providing a return on their investment. However, that is looking at our organizations via tunnel vision. It suggests that no entity outside those shareholders has any interest in the outcome of our business.

The other side of the coin is a much broader perspective on your organization. In 1984, Dr. Edward Freeman* suggested that there was another way to look at the organization. Freeman defined stakeholders as any entity that is either affected or can affect the business processes. This would include not only the shareholders but also the entire supply chain. When we change the direction of the discussion from shareholders to stakeholder, we now look at the organization from the total interaction within the business workplace. The stakeholders not only have a financial interest but they have an investment in the outcomes of the organization. It is a much clearer but harder-to-define view of the processes that govern the sustainability of your organization. The following exercise will clarify this stakeholder versus shareholder argument.

Who Is Going? (Suppliers, Inputs, Processes, Outputs, Customers)

The first tool we can utilize in this part of the process is a form referred to as a SIPOC. It demonstrates the suppliers, inputs, processes, outputs, and the end users of the business. It is applicable to every process within your organization. It provides a basic understanding of the flow through the

---

* http://www.corplaw.ie/blog/bid/317212/Shareholder-Stakeholder-Theories-Of-Corporate-Governance

organization. This same exercise can be applied to each of your suppliers within the supply chain as to how their output ends up as suppliers/inputs to your organization. For your process of understanding, the tool I have provided you below a copy of the form that is typically used in this identification effort.

SIPOC Diagram

Template Provided by Bright Hub Project Management

Suppliers	Input	Process	Output	Customers

Think back to the last trip you planned. Was part of the planning process to take into consideration who was going to go on this trip? Our journey is no different. From the outset, we need to determine exactly who is going on this journey. So I need you to take a moment, stop reading the text and think out of the box about who impacts your human resource (HR) processes. Let me expand that. Who impacts the process flow in your organization?

Exercise 2.1   Recruitment Process Sources—Suppliers

In order to simplify this journey somewhat, like we did in *Achieving HR Excellence through Six Sigma,* consider your recruitment process and identify your stakeholders in that process. Think out of the box.

_____

_____

_____

_____

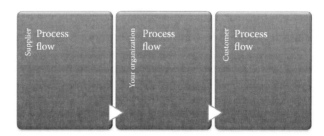

Figure 2.1 SIPOC.

How far out of the box did you go? Did you include only the usual suspects? Why did you choose that stakeholder? I fully realize that on the spur of the moment your list might not be as complete as if you took more time to contemplate your response. Considering this, let's return to your exercise and reconsider whom you added as suppliers in the recruitment process. Let me see if I can guide you a little bit (Figure 2.1). A supplier should be any person or group that provides something of value into the process. It is also critical that you remember that this same process occurs both before and after the material flow goes through your organization.

Exercise 2.2 Recruitment Process Sources—Inputs

Every stakeholder brings something to the table. Using your list or ours above, identify what each contributes to the recruitment process.

_____

_____

_____

Each supplier provides something to the recruitment process. These inputs establish the remainder of the process steps. Take a look at your recruitment process and see how these inputs fit into the bigger picture. Below is a further discussion of the way the process unfolds in your organization.

STEP 1: CREATION OF THE JOB REQUISITION

Where did you begin the process? It should have begun with the creation of a job requisition. In conjunction with the hiring manager, the HR department constructs a job requisition that details the key performance indicators (KPIs) for the position. These KPIs are the skills that both your organization and its customers have suggested are needed by someone fulfilling these duties and responsibilities. It is from the job requisition that the job notice is created and then dispersed out into the marketplace.

Let me present my list of responses to Exercise 2.1. How many of them matched your list? Did you have an identical list of players? If your list was different, why did you differ on the list?

Stakeholders of the Recruitment Process

- Hiring Manager
- Upper Management
- Chief Financial Officer
- Recruiter
- Candidate
- Current Employees
- Alumni Employees
- Reputation
- Vendors
- Clients
- Social Media
- Print Media
- Trade Associations
- Fellow Professionals
- Social Organizations
- Internet
- Consultants
- Chief HR Officer
- Local Colleges and Universities

STEP 2: WHAT DO THEY CONTRIBUTE TO THE PROCESS?

There is an old adage that states that every person we meet enters our life for a reason. This same adage can be applied to the sources that enter our recruitment process. Each and every one contribute, in some fashion, something to the process. The inputs tell the process where we go next. They create the steps of the process. It is critical that we identify those inputs, which are the critical few which lead to the success of the efforts of the organization. Let us return to my list and look at the inputs that they bring to the table. In the following exercise, what are the inputs brought by your sources list or mine as shown previously.

SOURCES FOR THE RECRUITMENT PROCESS AND THEIR INPUTS

- **Hiring Manager**—Identification of the need for the additional human capital assets based on workforce planning and/or work demand within the department. Their identification process includes the KPIs for success.

- **Upper Management**—Authorizes the hire in line with the strategic initiatives of the total organization.
- **Chief Financial Officer**—Responsible for ensuring that the benefit package falls within the parameters of the budgetary allotments of the organization. Ensures that the organization can afford the new headcount based on the revenues and liabilities in place at the time of hire.
- **Recruiter**—Through their activities they source, identify, and recruit the prospective new employees for consideration by the hiring manager and the HR department to fulfill the job requirements.
- **Candidates**—While they, as Allan Cox stated in his book *Confessions of a Corporate Headhunter,** are looking for the fast buck, they still bring the required skills and workplace behaviors to the organization.
- **Current Employees**—If we have engaged human capital assets, they are the first line of sources for prospective candidates from among their friends and peers.
- **Alumni Employees**—Just because an individual left your organization, does not mean that they will only tear the organization down. Look at LinkedIn and their list of groups. Almost every major organization has an alumni group. These individuals, like the current human capital assets, can be a great source for candidates for available openings.
- **Reputation**—Ever see the annual list of the best places to work for your location or nationally? These lists assist in establishing the employer of choice environment. The fact is that your organization on this list will bring candidates to your door based on their interest in working for an organization that reportedly cares about their human capital assets.
- **Vendors**—Assuming that your vendors are serving more than just your organization, they may know of potential candidates who might fill a position that you have open. They will come across other professionals in the same industry or similar industries in their travels.
- **Clients**—In the last book on which this guide is based, we advocated that the HR manager or director go out in the field with the top business development person at least once a quarter to visit the organization's clients. The purpose of the visit is to ask the client what attributes they expect from the human capital assets they deal with inside your organization. Their responses assist you in writing the job requisition because their wishes are the KPIs.
- **Social Media**—The involvement your organization has in the social media space will assist you in finding candidates. Using the discussion groups on LinkedIn, for example, will provide the vehicle for you to

---

* Alan Cox in his book written back in 1972 stated that a corporate headhunter is a mediator between executives who don't understand their problems and job candidates who don't care what the job is so long as there is a quick buck to be made.

discuss the attributes of your current human capital assets, which may be of interest to others.

- **Print Media**—Has a story appeared in your local newspaper about an expansion? Has a leading magazine written an article about your organization? Each of these is a source for the recruitment process.
- **Trade Associations**—Many trade associations maintain a job board on their website. The benefit of these candidates is that they are already within your industry and reportedly have the required skills you are seeking.
- **Fellow Professionals**—We are social animals. That means we like to talk with our peers in our chosen professionals. One of the areas that frequently comes into the discussion are the opportunities we may be aware of. If we have a strong presence in the workplace, these discussions could lead to the identification of the names of individuals who could fulfill our job openings.
- **Social Organizations**—Are you a member of the local country club? Are you a member of one of the local service organizations? Each provides you the opportunity to drop the idea that you are hiring for certain positions. There is a belief that many a business deal is completed on the golf course. This applies equally to the search for candidates.
- **Internet**—The Internet can bring you sources of candidates by the use of search engines for questions relating to what your organization does. If your organization is properly utilizing the search engine optimization (SEO) tools, your organization will come up higher on the search results, potentially leading to more people seeing what you do.
- **Consultants**—As a consultant, we are working with a number of organizations in a wide breadth of industries. It is through these activities that we may very well come across the individual who is the perfect match for your open requisition.
- **Chief HR Officer**—The Chief HR Officer has the obligation to the organization to ensure that each and every new hire, promotion or change within the organization is done with two directions in mind. The first is whether the HR action meets the budgetary constraints placed on the organization and second that we put the right person in the right job in the right place at the right time.
- **Local Colleges and Universities**—The business schools and the career services departments at many universities are a good source for interns, fresh graduates, and human capital assets working toward advanced degrees who could have an interest in your organization.

HOW DO WE GET THERE?—PROCESS MAP

To this point, we have looked at the sources that are responsible for the basics of our recruitment process. Each of these sources contributes something to the overall organizational structure. It is equally critical that you understand that inputs do not survive in a vacuum. They have to have some function. The inputs, therefore, become the basis for the process to which they are a part of.

Based on this premise, our next step is to get a picture of the overall process. This is typically done through the use of a process map. Using simple text boxes and arrows as connectors, the process map provides a 35,000-ft. level preview of the overall process. Each text box represents a step in the total process. I need to state at this point that no two recruitment process steps are going to be the same, so the steps I discuss here are generic in practice.

Exercise 2.3   Recruitment Processes

To this point you have reviewed your recruitment process and identified the entities that contribute the beginning of the supply chain, and we have looked at the contributions they have made in the form of inputs, which lead to processes. Considering your organization and reviewing the SIPOC, what processes are created?

_____

_____

_____

How many steps did you identify? If you went back and redid the process map would you add or delete any steps? Remember this is a high-level view of the process. Below is a discussion of the typical steps in a recruitment process.

BLOCK 1: POSITION OPENS UP

The process always begins with the evaluation of current human capital; management needs to determine where the organization may be falling short. The position typically opens due to a promotion, a retirement, an increased need for additional human capital assets, or a termination.

BLOCK 2: JOB DESCRIPTION REVIEW

The current job description is reviewed to determine whether it is a true picture of the current KPIs required to perform the duties of the position. It is also critical that the compensation package be reviewed to ensure that it is up to date and current with the organization benefits packages. The job description should be sent to the financial people to make sure it is within the current budget constraints.

BLOCK 3: HIRING MANAGER PREPARES JOB REQUISITION

Once the previous two steps are complete, the hiring manager sends the job requisition to the HR department to commence the search for the new talent. From the job description, the HR department transforms it into the format for distribution to the sources assisting with the search.

BLOCK 4: IDENTIFICATION OF INTERNAL PERSON RESPONSIBLE FOR THE SEARCH

The Chief HR Officer designates the internal staff recruiter who will be coordinating the search. They will be responsible for the sourcing, the identification and recruitment of candidates.

BLOCK 5: SOURCING FOR CANDIDATES COMMENCES

The assigned internal HR staff member begins the process of reaching out to the marketplace in search of prospective candidates. This would include the print media, social media, trade associations, external recruiters, area colleges, and local job services.

BLOCK 6: SELECTION OF CANDIDATES

As the candidate credentials are submitted, the internal HR department begins the process of screening the applications for comparison to the job requisition and job descriptions in order to identify those able to perform the bare essentials of the position's responsibilities.

BLOCK 7: SCHEDULING OF FIRST INTERVIEWS

From the selected candidates, the internal HR staff member begins to schedule interviews with an HR staff member to determine whether there is any further data point, which may further qualify them or disqualify them for the position.

BLOCK 8: FURTHER SCREENING

The selected HR staff member reviews the results of the first interviews to determine who the best candidates are to pass on to the next level of the process.

BLOCK 9: MANAGER INTERVIEWS

In conjunction with the hiring manager and the internal HR staff, the hiring manager schedules time to be set aside for the interview of the potential candidates for the position.

BLOCK 10: MANAGER SCREENINGS

Following the managerial interviews, the HR staff and hiring manager review the results of the interview process and determine who the best-fit candidates are and request that they return for the third interview. These interviews typically go more in-depth to their background and cultural fit to the organization. It may also involve behavioral interview panels and meetings with possible fellow workers.

BLOCK 11: THIRD INTERVIEW SCHEDULES

The third interviews are scheduled with the candidates and the organization.

BLOCK 12: FINAL SCREENINGS

The hiring manager collects all the results from the interviews and determines who best meets the requirements of the open requisition.

BLOCK 13: OFFER EXTENSION

The hiring manager sends to HR the name of the candidate who best meets the requirement. HR in turn extends to the candidate the offer based on the desires of the hiring manager.

BLOCK 14: OFFER ACCEPTANCE

The candidate accepts the offer or a feedback loop runs back to the beginning of the process if the candidate rejects the offer for any reason.

BLOCK 15: PREEMPLOYMENT SCREENING

Following the acceptance of the offer, the organization begins the process of completing the screening of the potential employee. This includes the background checks, I-9 verification, and checking references. This may be done by an outside vendor who specializes in doing background checks as part of their services.

BLOCK 16: NEW EMPLOYEE REPORTS FOR WORK

Following a successful screening, the new employee sets a start date and handles the paperwork required for them to be up and running in your organization.

BLOCK 17: FIRST DAY OF WORK

Employee enters the on-boarding process and meets with the hiring manager to establish organizational policies and procedures.

The next step in the SIPOC is a review of what the process creates. Every process has as an end product the creation of something. If the suppliers have contributed inputs to the organization, which have created processes, what do those processes supply to the organization?

Exercise 2.4 Recruitment Process Outputs

To this point you have reviewed your recruitment process and identified the entities that contribute to the beginning of the supply chain, and we have looked at the contributions they have made in the form of inputs, which lead to processes. Considering your organization and reviewing the SIPOC, what outputs are created?

_____

_____

_____

Consider this equation. With every contribution that a supplier makes to the organization, there is something imputed to the process. From the process, the results of the process create an action or output that comes out the other side of the process. This output is usually in the form of some product or service we deliver to the ultimate end user.

What Do They Want—Voice of the Customer

Exercise 2.5 Recruitment Process Customers

To this point you have reviewed your recruitment process and identified the entities that contribute the beginning of the supply chain, and we have looked at the contributions they have made in the form of inputs, which lead to processes. Considering your organization and reviewing the customers, what are they telling you they need to satisfy their demands?

_____

_____

_____

Do you really know what your customers want? The purpose of this chapter has been to see the problem facing your organization. We think we have a problem but it is not crystal clear at this point exactly what that problem is. If you have a problem, the customer is the primary source of the root cause of the problem (Figure 2.2).

Allow me to simplify it for you. The problem is a representation of the gap between what you are currently doing and what the customer is willing to pay for. Nothing more. Nothing less. The customer tells us their demands via the *voice of the customer*. If we are meeting those demands, the organization is running well. If they are not, and most are not, then there is a problem that needs to be resolved. The ultimate method for judging the voice of the customer is through the use of the voice of the customer matrix as shown previously.

In any given organization, the goal is to deliver the product or service faster, better, and cheaper than our competition.

When we refer to better, we are meaning that the process step is completed with as few errors in the process as possible. Rework is waste. Rework means that we are not meeting the needs of the customer. Especially in the HR function, rework can be detrimental financially when we recruit the wrong individual for that open position. It is the basic metric that if we incorrectly hire an individual for a position it will take us 175% of the failed hire's salary to replace them.

			Plan			Develop			Market			Deliver		Support			
	Customer requirements	Importance (1–5)	Internal consultant	Customer surveys	X functional team	Internal controls	Talent screening	Dept. partnerships	Policies	Procedures	Process	Sourcing vehicles	Talent search	Employment offers	Preinterview steps	Prehire steps	Onboarding
Better	Treat me like you want my business	5	1	2	2	4	2	4	4	2	2	2	2	2	1	1	2
	Deliver services that meet my needs	5	2	2	2	2	2	2	2	2	2	2	2	2	2	2	2
	Services that work right	3	2	2	2	1	2	2	2	2	2	2	2	2	2	2	2
	Be accurate, right the first time	4	2	2	2	1	2	2	2	2	2	2	2	2	2	2	2
	Source us the right candidate	5	2	2	2	1	2	2	2	2	2	2	2	2	2	2	2
Faster	I want it when I want it	3	2	2	2	1	2	2	2	2	2	1	2	2	4	2	2
	Make commitments that meet my needs	4	2	2	2	1	2	2	2	2	2	2	2	2	4	2	2
	Meet your commitments	4	2	2	2	1	2	2	2	2	2	2	2	2	4	2	2
	I want fast, easy access to help	4	2	2	2	1	2	2	2	2	2	2	2	2	2	2	2
	Do not waste my time	5	2	2	2	1	2	2	2	2	2	2	2	2	2	2	2
	If it breaks, fix it fast	4	2	2	2	1	2	2	2	2	2	2	2	2	2	2	2
Cheaper	Deliver irresistable value	4	2	2	2	1	4	2	2	2	2	2	2	1	2	2	2
	Help me save money	5	4	2	2	1	4	2	2	2	2	2	2	1	2	2	2
	Help me save time	5	4	2	2	1	4	2	2	2	2	2	2	1	2	2	1
	Total Weight		135	120	120	80	148	130	130	120	120	117	120	106	137	115	115

Legend: ● 4 Strong; ○ 2 Medium; △ 1 Weak. Business functions. Voice of the Customer.

Figure 2.2 Voice of the customer matrix.

When we refer to faster, we mean can we meet the needs or demands of the client before they need it and done correctly based on their specifications. Finally, if we can do it with less rework and faster, can we also deliver it at a lower overall cost than the client was expecting?

Let me walk you through the operation of the matrix. The matrix is divided into both horizontal and vertical columns. To begin the process of completing the matrix, we begin with the vertical column. The vertical column is divided into better, faster, and cheaper. In each segment, we want to record what your customer tells you are their requirements to meet the three goals. Each segment provides you room to record the customer's most critical needs. For example, in the better category notice the vertical column refers to treat me like you want my business, delivering services that meet my needs, services that work right the first time, delivery is on time, and we found them the right candidate in a search.

Turn to the horizontal section of the matrix. It consists of a number of columns, each serving a specific purpose. The first column provides a space to record the importance of the customer requirements. This is done on a numerical score of 1–5 with 5 being of the most important. The second column represents the presence of the internal consultant. The rest of the horizontal columns represent the various stages of the project life cycle. We begin with the planning stage in which we first plan out the project followed by the development of the process steps. These two lead to how we market the service, deliver it, and what support we are going to provide after the delivery.

The next step is the critical part of the matrix. You need to first rate the requirements as previously stated on a scale of 1–5 as to their importance to the overall success of the client requirements. The rest of the columns relate to the various stages and these are developed based on the block in the upper left-hand corner of the matrix. The box asks the individual or individuals to determine whether the needs are of a strong nature, a medium nature, or a weak nature. These are represented by the numerals 4, 2, 1. The appropriate numeral is placed in each box.

The key to the usage of the matrix is the formulation of the weighted averages. They are calculated by multiplying the importance level by the business importance. When you add up the columns at the bottom, it enables you to identify the critical few actions that your organization needs to work on. We do this by choosing the 3–5 highest weighted averages.

What Is Missing?

I began this chapter indicating our preplanning was all about seeing the problem. At this point, we have partially reached that goal. We began by identifying the stakeholders of our process and what they contribute to our organization. Following the identification process, we turned to taking a high-level view of the organization through our creation of the process map of the recruitment process. Finally, we completed the "voice of the customer" matrix.

If we go back and look at the process map of the current recruitment process and compare it to the requirements that the client has set down, there will appear some very definitive differences.

These definitive differences represent the first part of the TLS Continuum. It is with the assistance of the tools from the *theory of constraints* that we are able to get a handle on what obstacles are in the current process state, which is holding up the ability of your organization to meet the demands of the customer without the presence of nonvalued activities.

The theory of constraints offers us an additional tool to assist us in critically thinking about the problems facing our processes. Dr. Eliyahu Goldratt called it an *evaporating cloud*. Its sole purpose is to relieve conflict from the system.

The evaporating cloud begins with the problem at hand. From there it looks at the reasons why the organization can't resolve the issue. The evaporating cloud diagram contains two tracts. The upper tract gives the reasons why we need to take certain actions to improve the problem while the lower track presents the reasons why the organization can't achieve the resolution to the problem.

Reading from left to right we begin with the objective (o), which is the solution the team has determined will most likely resolve the obstacle we discovered in the fishbone. The remainder of the evaporating cloud looks at both the perquisites and the requirements to meet the goal.

The evaporating cloud diagram is read in the following manner. Our goal (reducing excessive hire time) is referred to as "A" or the goal. In order to have the goal, we need to have requirement 1. In order to have requirement 1, we need to have prerequisite 1.

The lower track is read the same way (Figure 2.3).

The theory of constraints process provides us direction as to what to change, what to change it to, and how to make the change happen. To better understand the process, consider the evaporating cloud example shown earlier.*

Let me walk you through the cloud. The head of the cloud is the goal (A). In this case that goal is to locate the talent we want to fill critical HR

---

* Taken from an article written for *Mobility* magazine in 2001: http://dbaiconsulting.com/Articles /Articale9.pdf

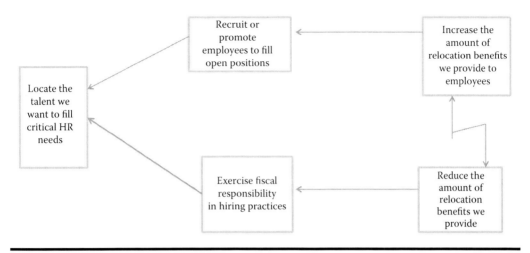

Figure 2.3   Evaporating cloud.

needs. The organization feels that there is sufficient justification to add headcount to the organization in order to fulfill the need for human capital assets in key areas within the organization.

So, the follow-up question is, what do we need to have in place in order to meet that goal? This becomes the requirement for the cloud. In our previous example, we are confronted with two different reactions to the problem or the goal. The first requirement is stated that in order to locate the talent needed to fill the critical HR needs of the organization we must either promote from within or go outside the organization to find the individuals. At the same time, the financial people are stating that this is fine but we must remain fiscally in line with the organization and not exceed the budgeted amounts for recruitment. Do you begin to see the conflict forming? These two tracks represent P1 and P2 in the cloud interpretation.

In order to meet the requirements of the goal, we need to have in place certain conditions. These conditions play the role of the prerequisites and are required to be in place prior to achieving our goal. Once again the two tracks fail to meet in the middle. One response as to the prerequisites states that in order to recruit or promote new talent within the organization, we must increase the benefits offered. The other side says we must reduce the benefit levels to recruit the required new talent.

The two prerequisite boxes are joined by a jagged line, which represents the organizational conflict. It asks the organization to make the determination, which is more important in the long run: Not taking risks and remaining penny-wise, or do we do what is needed to get the talent we need?

Exercise 2.6 Recruitment Process—Evaporating Cloud

Think of your own organization. Are there any problems that you are experiencing that you can plainly delineate the two conflicting paths as described in the preceeding example? Explain the two paths.

_____

_____

_____

YOUR TICKET TO RIDE—THE PROJECT CHARTER*

To summarize what I have presented in this preplanning stage, we have arrived at the "airport" determined to begin this unique journey even though we have no idea of where we are going.

As in any journey we have established who is going (the stakeholders). I looked at the role these stakeholders play in the issue confronting your organization. They are stakeholders because they contribute something to the overall recruiting process. This contribution may be in the form of knowledge or a physical contribution. We have looked at what the customer is telling the organization as to what they expect from us. We have looked at how the process works on a daily basis. The difference between the current state of the process and the demands (requirements) of the customer create our problem. It creates the area where you must concentrate your efforts on in process improvement.

With the obstacles identified I moved to the goal tree. It tells us if we identify the problem (goal) then there are certain operational factors that must be in place to get us to the solution. The most efficient way to track these efforts is through the use of a Six Sigma methodology tool we call a project charter.

In *Achieving HR Excellence through Six Sigma*, we went through a typical charter statement in simple terms. Look at the following form and I will cover it in more detail.

---

* The Project Charter Form is the one utilized by the St. Petersburg College Six Sigma training program.

Project Name/Title:				
Sponsoring Organization:				
Project Sponsor:				

Team Members (Name)	Role

Principal Stakeholder	Proposed Benefit

Sponsor Approval Signature / Date:

Preliminary Plan (Milestones)		Target Date	Actual Date	Approvals

Project Name/Title:
Problem / Opportunity Statement
Project Goal: Solution/Recommendation
Resources Requested (What you need, $, personnel, time, etc.)
Project Impact Statement

SECTION 1: THE PROJECT NAME/TITLE

This is the departure point of our journey. It requires a definitive statement as to what the problem is. It should be a complete sentence and provide the organization with some indication of where you are headed.

SECTION 2: SPONSORING ORGANIZATION

Self-explanatory—this should be the name of your organization or department in which the problem has been uncovered.

SECTION 3: PROJECT SPONSOR

The process improvement efforts do not exist in a vacuum. There must be someone within the organization who most benefits from the solution to the problem. This individual must be willing to be the gatekeeper for the project effort and to run interference with those who might want to derail the effort. They are the ones who must go to upper management and insist that the success of the organization is dependent on this project being successful.

SECTION 4: TEAM MEMBERS

I have talked earlier about these projects being cross-functional in nature. Therefore, the very important first step is to look at your organization. If your problem, as I have suggested, is recruiting-related what departments are affected by your project?

Exercise 2.7   Project Team

You have determined that there are some problems in the way the organization recruits new talent that results in longer than normal time to fill. Which departments might be affected? Who would you place on the project team?

_____

_____

_____

_____

If your project team is constructed properly, there should be a representative of each of the departments mentioned in Exercise 2.7 as part of the team. The members need to be representative of the affected areas with freedom to contribute to discussion in a meaningful way.

SECTION 5: PRINCIPAL STAKEHOLDER

In the beginning of this chapter, I spent some time talking about who the stakeholders represent. Normally, there is one stakeholder who stands above the rest as to the benefits of the outcomes. It is critical that you identify these parties.

Once you have identified the primary stakeholder, the next step is to identify the benefit the stakeholder has in the completion of your project. How is your organization going to be different following the completion of the project?

SECTION 6: SPONSOR APPROVAL

I mentioned earlier the role of the sponsor and while it is a vital one they have one other task as part of this effort. They in essence have to put their mouth where they say it is by signing off on the project, giving organizational approval to move forward.

SECTION 7: PRELIMINARY MILESTONES

I began this book with the concept that we were on a unique journey, one with a beginning but no end. That does not mean that the journey can go on forever without some time restraints. We begin the project and along the way we reach a point where it makes sense to distribute information about our progress. These points become milestones in the project. In my black belt project for instance, the milestones consisted of the following:

- Determining the scope of the project
- Preparing and submitting the project charter
- Determining the evaluation methods
- Analyze the training data
- Construct the dashboards
- Construct the balance scorecard
- Deliver the final product to the stakeholders

In each case, the milestone must determine a target date for the delivery of each milestone. The project charter also provides a space for showing the actual date the milestone was delivered. It is also a necessity that each milestone is signed off from the rest of the project by someone eligible to do so.

SECTION 8: PROJECT TITLE

It is simply a repeat of the information in Step 1 as this is the beginning of page 2 of the charter.

SECTION 9: PROBLEM/OPPORTUNITY STATEMENT

The problem/opportunity statement section allows us space to further explain what the problem is and the benefits of resolving the issues. It represents a full paragraph description of the issue and the background information surrounding the problem. It is designed to further explain what we expect to achieve in the process.

SECTION 10: PROJECT GOAL

In the first book, we discussed the fact that the Six Sigma methodology is an adult version of the scientific method you discussed in high-school science classes. This section represents the hypothesis part of the experiment. It is in this section that we begin to explain what we think will come out from the issue exploration we are about to begin.

SECTION 11: RESOURCES REQUESTED

Every process project will require certain things to succeed. It will need personnel to form the cross-functional teams; it will need funds to conduct the experiments; it will require time from the regular day-to-day operations away from their home responsibilities.

Each resource needs to be detailed with the particulars surround it. If you are including human capital assets, then you need to include what hours and pay will be involved.

SECTION 12: PROJECT IMPACT STATEMENT

This final and probably the most important section of the project charter is the space for you to explain what outcome you expect. It should include specific metrics if they are available or expected.

For instance, using our recruitment process, I could word a project impact statement as "It is our expectation that through the implementation of (name of the solution) we can expect that the time to hire will be reduced by 60 percent to 45 days from 75 days." Take note that we were very specific in the anticipated outcomes.

In the next chapter, we will begin the next phase of the journey. We will have departed and begun the final four steps of DMAIC (define, measure, analyze, improve, and control) process.

Chapter 3

Flight to Excellence

> Good morning ladies and gentlemen, this is your captain speaking. I want to welcome you aboard TLS Continuum Flight 2014 service from your current location to an unknown destination. Once we get airborne today, our flight time will be 14 hours; we are expecting some turbulence on the way so we will leave the seat belt lights on for the duration of the trip.[*]

In the previous chapter, I presented the same process steps, as we would undertake in planning a family vacation. We established who was going on the trip (SIPOC) and we established the family wishes (Voice of the Customer Matrix) and we laid out our trip agenda (the process map).

The next stage is the actual trip. It is our road to human resource (HR) excellence. By comparing the three elements mentioned earlier, I have provided the clues in order for you to see the problem. However, there is one more element we need to consider. The difference between what the Voice of Customer Matrix tells us our customers are willing to pay for and the process map, which tells us the current state of how we do things within the organization; we can identify the process obstacles.

---

[*] The dialogue is taken from a sample captain's speech found on the website http://airodyssey.net /reference/inflight/

Ishikawa Fishbone—Why We Do Things*

Dr. Kaoru Ishikawa

Dr. Kaoru Ishikawa of the University of Tokyo created the fishbone tool in 1943. The purpose of the tool is to look at the root causes within our operations that create nonvalue added activities.

Exercise 3.1   Ishikawa Fishbone

You have determined that there are some problems in the way the organization recruits new talent that results in longer than normal time to fill an open position. Why is the extended hire time a problem for the organization?

_____

_____

_____

_____

The Ishikawa diagram begins with the head or the process effect. The fish head defines the problem. Consider the example in Exercise 3.1, where you have been tasked to explain why the organization is experiencing longer than normal time to fill an open position. The head (effect) of the fishbone diagram would indicate that the effect on the organization would be the longer than normal hire time. Your next task is to identify both the primary and secondary causes of the problem.

Primary causes are comprised of those causes that have a direct bearing on the cause categories. They are usually supplemented with an additional cause that contributes to our primary causes. For example, if we have a longer than normal time to hire, the primary cause might be that our job criteria are too restrictive. The secondary cause might be that we have too restrictive job criteria because we have not identified the key performance indicators of the position correctly.

Returning to our fishbone diagram, following the identification of the obstacle or the effect of the process, we find that the remainder of the

_____

* https://www.moresteam.com/toolbox/fishbone-diagram.cfm

fishbone diagram represents the causes of the problem. It is the purpose of the fishbone diagram for us to identify the causes of the obstacle from an eagle's view. Each of these causes is represented by an arm or bone of the diagram. Typically the arms are represented by a standard nomenclature of the causality. Typically the Ishikawa fishbone is comprised of the following high-level causes:

Cause 1: Management

Exercise 3.2   Ishikawa Fishbone

Considering that you have determined that the obstacle you discovered was an extended hiring time, how has management contributed to the obstacle?

_____

_____

_____

_____

Management has a rough road to travel. They need to think about the human capital assets of the organization as well as the demands of the stakeholders as we saw earlier in our discussion regarding the SIPOC tool. Taking all this into consideration, management can either be your friend or your worst nightmare. Before we continue our explanation of the Ishikawa diagram, we need to consider this dilemma more in depth.

The website Dictionary.com defines an enemy as "a person who feels hatred for, fosters harmful designs against, or engages in antagonistic activities against another, an adversary or opponent."[*] Many managers have been brought up through the ranks of the organization ingrained with the focus that their job is to tell the organization when something needs to be done and how to do it. There is no room for alternative solutions.

If your management is so ingrained in this belief and the expectation that they will follow like sheep, then the system falls apart. When this

---

* http://dictionary.reference.com/browse/enemy?s=t

management philosophy is the guiding principle of the organization, management tends to be stuck in this rut; the tendency is to throw up additional obstacles to the process. It also means that the effort to remove the process obstacles is doomed to fail.

Look at these scenarios to illustrate my point:

Scenario #1: The hiring manager calls your office and tells you that he/she needs a particular position filled in 3 days. You go out and source the candidates, screen them and present them to the manager and he sits on them for a week. What happened to the 3-day window?

Scenario #2: The hiring manager calls your office and tells you that he/she needs a particular position filled in 3 days. You go out and source the candidates, screen them, and present them to the manager and he/she asks to see all the resumes plus he wants to do his/her own search for the right talent to fill the position. What happened to the 3-day window?

Consider the reverse of the preceding work environment. In this alternative work environment, your management is able to see the problem and feel its direct impact on the organization. Management understands that sustainability and innovation of the organization are at risk because there are process steps within your organization that are halting progress. The problem here is that even though they understand the problem, in many cases they may not recognize the event that is part of the problem. Consider this scenario:*

> An organization discovered that in the process of hiring a middle management executive the job requisition is reviewed and approved three times. As a former executive recruiter that is not necessarily a problem. However, as the late Paul Harvey used say—the rest of the story is that in the process of hiring that middle management executive, the job requisition is reviewed and approved by the same person.

If that executive has other items on his desk, that requisition approval may take longer than it should, resulting in a longer time to hire.

In many cases, the organization operates from a top-down perspective, so if your managers are not totally bought into the concept of process improvement, this can create a major obstacle to reaching the goal stated in our fish head.

---

* In the course of a 2-day seminar we facilitate based on the book *Achieving HR Excellence*, the scenario became apparent in the course of completing a Value Stream Map.

Cause 2: People

Exercise 3.3 Ishikawa Fishbone

Considering that you have determined that the obstacle you discovered was an extended hiring time, how have people contributed to the obstacle?

_____

_____

_____

_____

We are all subject to human nature. The fishbone diagram head says that we have an excessive time to hire. Our response is based in human nature. The people part of the equation will base their response to the excessive time to hire in terms of WIIFM or "What's in it for me." Their decisions on the obstacle will be centered on what effect the cure of the obstacle would have on them not only in the future but also in the present. Consider this scenario:

The preceding steps have determined that the time to hire is excessive for the organization to function at a successful level. Some of your human capital assets will look at this scenario and conclude that the reduction in time to hire will benefit them due to the increased manpower available to handle process steps. If there are more hands on deck then the conclusion can be made that they will not have to work as many long hours. Look at the other side of the coin. Some human capital assets on the other hand will consider the excessive time to hire as a boon to them because if it takes longer to hire new talent, then that opens the opportunity for some overtime work. This overtime will lead to more dollars in their pockets, which means their families benefit from the extra discretionary income.

Cause 3: Method

Exercise 3.4   Ishikawa Fishbone

Considering that you have determined that the obstacle you discovered was an extended hiring time, how has the process contributed to the obstacle?

_____

_____

_____

_____

Lynne Hambleton in her book *Treasure Chest of Six Sigma Growth Methods, Tools, and Best Practices* describes method as the way we do things, which could be misunderstood or incomplete.[*] If the process of hiring a new human capital asset is not straightforward, there is a potential for our head of the fishbone diagram to be a problem. Consider something as simple as the job requisition stating that the hire must take place within 3 days. Is that 3 calendar days or 3 business days? In most cases, it will not be as simplistic as the example in the previous sentence.

The method maybe unclear on intent or it maybe unclear because the parties involved have not received the proper guidance on how the process is supposed to work. Our intent with all processes is that they must be designed in such a way as to show a direct correlation between the process step and the removal of the obstacle. These steps must reflect our intent to meet the total voice of the customer with little or no defects along the way. Many organizations today still require a hard copy of the application even though the same information is stored in the applicant tracking system.

---

[*] Hambleton, Lynne. *Treasure Chest of Six Sigma Growth Methods, Tools, and Best Practices.* New York, NY: Prentice Hall, 2008, p. 175.

Cause 4: Measurement

Exercise 3.5   Ishikawa Fishbone

Considering that you have determined that the obstacle you
discovered was an extended hiring time, how has measurement
contributed to the obstacle?

_____

_____

_____

_____

We understand, as stated in *Achieving HR Excellence through Six Sigma*,
that we can't question what we don't measure. But there are times when
the way we measure or how we measure things can be a detriment to
the process. Returning to our obstacle of excessive hire time, if we take
too long to conduct the measurement we risk the possibility of losing our
key talent prospects. If our key performance indicators are too restrictive, the measurement may eliminate key candidates. It becomes critical
that we ensure that we are using the right measurement tools for the right
situation.

McCarty, Daniels, Bremer, and Gupta in their *Six Sigma Black Belt
Handbook*[*] state that the project team needs to verify the measurement system they are using before collecting data; the measurement obstacle should be addressed initially before tackling other
root causes.

_____

[*] McCarty, Tom et al. *The Six Sigma Black Belt Handbook.* New York, NY: McGraw Hill, 2005.
p. 366.

Cause 5: Machine

Exercise 3.6 Ishikawa Fishbone

Considering that you have determined that the obstacle you discovered is an extended hiring time, how has technology contributed to the root cause?

_____

_____

_____

_____

There is a big push in the corporate world to automate everything. But these efforts are routed in some kind of machine and they tend to do some strange things at times. It is critical that we understand the role that technology plays in our organization along with the really viable fallacies in its use.

There is a considerable debate going currently regarding the move toward "big data" within the HR function. Big data is focused on the manipulation of large amounts of measurements, which are centered in the technology used by the organization. While the Ishikawa diagram asks us to look at the causes of the obstacles, big data is more interested in the correlation of events.

Consider the following example:

> The organization is in a hiring mode. The problem they see is not one of excessive hiring time but rather one in which a particular manager seems to be continually hiring the wrong human capital asset. The difference in the two approaches can clearly be found in an analysis of the scenario.

First, from a big data perspective, there is a tool called predicative analysis. Predictive Analysis World defines predictive analysis as "a business intelligence technology that produces a predictive score for each customer or other organizational element. Assigning these predictive scores is the job of a predictive model, which has, in turn been trained over your data, learning from the experience of your organization."[*] In simpler terms,

---

[*] http://www.predictiveanalyticsworld.com/predictive_analytics.php

technology has been asked to review your data to identify those events from a historical basis which states that if manager A is the one that is conducting the interview, there is a good chance that he/she will continue to produce a bad hire because of the record of past hires. The primary focus is the correlation with events as an indicator of the obstacle (e.g., excessive hire time) occurring.

Second, we use the same scenario, but we are now concerned with whether or not there are some underlying cause that is the reason why this manager has problems in hiring the right human capital asset. Is the candidate profile flawed? Is the candidate telling us one thing on the application but telling the manager something else?

We need to be sure that our technology is measuring the right metrics and in the right way to meet the needs of the HR function and the organization as a whole.

Cause 6: Material

Exercise 3.7 Ishikawa Fishbone

Considering that you have determined that the obstacle you discovered was an extended hiring time, how has material contributed to the obstacle?

_____

_____

_____

_____

When we refer to materials, we are talking about the various things we expect the candidates and managers to input into the system. This could be the application or it could be the interview rating form. These may be embedded in your applicant tracking system or it may be a hard copy, which ends up in their employee file if hired. The excessive hiring time could be caused by errors in any of the forms used in the process.

In a recent conversation with Steven Bonacorsi,* he stated that Kaoru Ishikawa never liked the term "diagram," considering it too flat in nature. The true value of the exercise utilized by Kaoru Ishikawa is the use of the "5 whys." It is a series of questions preceded by the word "why." Looking at the drilldown to the root cause effecting the Y output of the Ishikawa diagram as follows (Figure 3.1):

In the preceding fishbone, we observe that the problem is extended hiring time. So the process works as follows:

Why Question 1: Why do we have high employee turnover? Through some brainstorming and input from management, we find that one of the reasons might be the location of your facility.

Why Question 2: Why is location a problem? The response to the question will create a secondary why question opportunity.

Why Question 3: If location is a problem, why is it a problem? In the preceding example, the response is that location is a problem because it is hard to drive to.

Why Question 4: Why is it hard to drive to? We have a client who found this problem in their hiring process, where they would bring in a candidate for an interview and schedule a return trip in almost the same day. The plant is located 2 hours from the airport. To schedule the interview

---

* Steven Bonacorsi is the president at the International Standard for Lean Six Sigma (ISLSS) and a Master Six Sigma Black Belt.

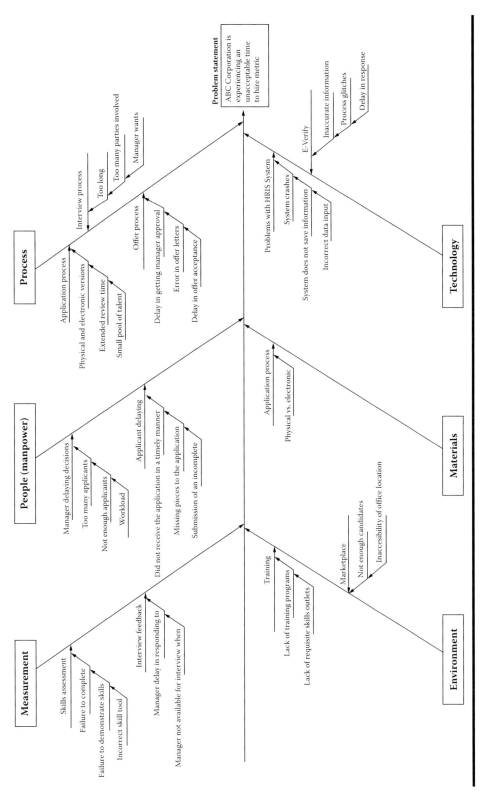

Figure 3.1   Ishikawa fishbone examples.

process in 1 day was a problem. The preceding fishbone tells you that the response is because the facility is in a small town or in a rural location.

This process can be carried out through the rest of the bones of the diagram in much the same way. It is important to understand the tool only works when your responses to the Why questions are not the solutions but rather the reason why the particular element contributes to the causes and effects of the issue at hand. In addition the major categories of the obstacle causes are not set in stone. You may Google the term "Ishikawa fishbone" and you will see many people include other causes such as environment to describe the workplace.

SUPERCHARGE THE EAGLE'S VIEW

Exercise 3.8   The Value Stream Map

> In Chapter 2, we asked you to block out your recruitment process, which we referred to as a process map. This exercise takes the process map to the next step. Take out your process map along with a fresh sheet of paper. On the new sheet between each step of the process map, insert the time increments between each stage along with every decision, document, and movement action that occurs. Include any additional actions, which take place between each stage.

_____

_____

_____

_____

Before we continue a word of caution, do not begin this process unless you are willing to devote the time to it. The process of creating a value stream map is labor intensive and takes some use of critical thinking. By time we are referring to at a minimum of at least an hour.

The purpose behind the process map is to give you a view of your organizational process from an eagle's point of view. It is looking down on the organization and seeing an overall view of how the process works. The purpose of the value stream map is to bring your focus down to the office floor. Our actions do not operate in a vacuum but are interdependent on the rest of the organization. The act of creating the value stream map involves taking our process map and expanding it. The expanded view contains every time lapse, every document, every decision, and so forth.

Take the initial block we discussed in Chapter 2: we began the discussion of the process map with stating that the recruitment process begins with the opening of a job position within the organization. This is followed by a review of the job description for the position to ensure that it is current.

To complete the value stream map, look at these first two steps. We first determine how long we need to allocate to the review process. Is it several hours or is it several days? Once we have determined the allotted time, we then need to look at all the other actions required to complete the review. This would include the writing of any documents, any phone conversations required, any e-mails that need to be sent and responded to. The determination of the time allotment needs to incorporate all these actions.

The same procedures must be undertaken for each step of the process map. The final product of the value stream map, while containing the same steps as the process map, is entirely different in appearance.

HOW ARE WE GOING TO GET THERE?—THE GOAL TREE[*]

It is critical that we make sure we are on the same page at this juncture. We began by looking at the SIPOC tool. It gave us the insight as to who the stakeholders are. Remember we are interested in more than those with a strictly financial interest in our organization. The stakeholders provided us the data points regarding what they bring to the table in the course of delivering our services or products.

From the SIPOC, I asked you to develop a high-level process map of the recruiting process within your organization. There were many potential HR processes we could have chosen to work with; however, the recruitment is the one with the most universal applicability. When complete, the process map demonstrates what steps the process requires to meet the needs of the organization.

Next, we turned to the Voice of the Customer Matrix. The voice of the customer is the critical basis for enabling the organization to move forward. It tells us what factors the customer needs in order to substantiate their organizational investment in ours.

If you have put enough thought into your process maps, the difference between your current state process and the client's requirements creates a clear picture of where your roadblocks or obstacles are. It is these obstacles that characterize your problem. The next step, therefore, is to lay out the journey itinerary, if you will. What steps are we going to take to try and get to that end destination, as nebulous as it is?

We can do this through the use of Dettmer's Goal Tree.[†]

---

[*] The Goal Tree is a concept introduced by William Dettmer in his book *Goldratt's Theory of Constraints* published in 1997 by the American Society for Quality. The concept was further refined in his sequel *The Logical Thinking Process* published in 2007.

[†] Dettmer, William. *The Logical Thinking Process.* Milwaukee, WI: ASQ Press, 2007, pp. 72–88.

The Goal Tree clearly lays out that road map. Look at Figure 3.1 as it visually presents the road map as we walk through it. The Goal Tree requires you systematically review the problem. It begins with looking at the goal or your anticipated solutions. It not only asks you what the intended solutions are but also it asks you to take the search a step further (Figure 3.2).

Exercise 3.9   Goal Tree—Goal/Objective

Remaining with your recruiting process, what is the goal or objective of the process? Think about it carefully. Have you carried out your thought process to its fullest extent?

_____

_____

_____

_____

Once you have established the objective, you must then take the next step and determine what has to be present in order for you achieve that goal. These represent the critical success factors; without their presence you can't reach that goal.

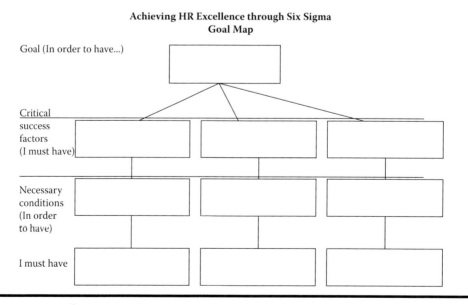

Figure 3.2   Goal Tree.

Exercise 3.10   Goal Tree—Critical Success Factors

> Remaining with your recruiting process, having established your goal or objective, what factors will establish whether you were successful or not? Think about it carefully. Have you carried out your thought process to its fullest extent?

_____

_____

_____

_____

The critical success factors section of the Goal Tree asks you to determine the three factors that you have to have in place in order to determine that you have the right solution. It poses the question that in order to reach the solution I must have these critical success factors in place. It is absolutely critical that you carry your identification of these three factors to the widest audience possible. Like the goal statement, the first factor that may come to mind may not be the best possible concept.

The Goal Tree then moves down the hierarchy to the next level. It is in this factor that you ask yourself further questions regarding the process. Follow me here a bit.

You began the completion of the Goal Tree by asking the question, what is the solution for the problem at hand? Then your next question is what are the critical success factors, which will indicate that we have reached that goal? These are the factors that must be there in order for us to reach that goal. This is not the end of the process, however.

Exercise 3.11   Goal Tree—Conditions

> Remaining with your recruiting process, what are the necessary conditions that will lead you to the critical success factors? Think about it carefully. Have you carried out your thought process to its fullest extent?

_____

_____

_____

_____

Think of it in this fashion. In order to have (goal) I must have (critical success factors). In order to create the critical success factors, I must have (necessary conditions).

If you know what the goal is and you know what critical success factors equal success, what has to be present to reach that level? Consider once again the recruitment process. Our goal is to provide the organization with the human capital assets that will enhance the output of the organization in the form of products and services. If I am correct in this goal, then what are the necessary critical success factors? I would suggest that they are the location of the right person, in the right place, at the right time.

In order to achieve this state, the necessary conditions become the establishment of a working system to source, identify, and recruit these critical human capital assets that are needed by the organization to sustain it through the years to come.

Exercise 3.12   Goal Tree—Knowledge

Remaining with your recruiting process, what is the necessary knowledge that will lead you to the necessary conditions? Think about it carefully. Have you carried out your thought process to its fullest extent?

_____

_____

_____

_____

In Chapter 1 during our discussion regarding the characteristics of a "center of excellence," we talked about one of the characteristics of the center was the gaining of knowledge and resources. This process is not one that we can conduct in a fly-by-night fashion. We need to understand why the system requires us to do what we do. The final stage of the Goal Tree is to determine what knowledge resources are required to form the basis for the rest of the tree.

Chapter 4

Layover—Obstacles to Improvement

> Ladies and gentlemen, the captain has turned on the fasten seat belt sign. We are now crossing a zone of turbulence. Please return to your seats and place your seats in the upright position and keep your seat belts fastened. We also ask that you secure your tray tables. Thank you.[*]

Our continued journey is going to be everything but smooth sailing. In the preceding scenario it is equivalent to the turbulence that an airplane might encounter when it hits rough weather in the course of a flight. I am not unmindful that some of you have read this book with great trials and tribulations. You have come from a world that is embedded in a tradition, which says that is not the way we do things here. Some of you have been confronted by organizations very much adverse to doing things differently. You have been the victims of command and control organizational structures (Figure 4.1).

Know and understand it has to change. Human beings tend to resist change. It is not that we will not change when we have to, but our first preference is not to have to. The way to ease this turbulence is to be able to demonstrate first why we have to make the change, and second how is it going to affect us. This includes both pros and cons of the anticipated change.

---

[*] The dialogue is taken from a sample captain's speech found on the website http://airodyssey.net /reference/inflight/

Figure 4.1   Bull in the china shop.

Typically this turbulence occurs in the change process under four primary reasons or excuses, as the followings:

Excuse 1: It Is a Manufacturing Thing

I will fully agree that the continuous process improvement efforts began on the factory floor. They were designed to remove defects from the manufacturing process. However, our nonmanufacturing operations within the same organization still undergo the production of defects. Take a moment and consider the next exercise.

Exercise 4.1   It's a Manufacturing Thing

Six Sigma was created on the factory floor and some state that means that it will not work in the service side of the business. Do you agree or disagree and why?

_____

_____

_____

_____

Yes, it is correct that the Theory of Constraints–Lean–Six Sigma (TLS) Continuum came out of the factory floor. However, we are not talking about producing something per se. We are talking about a way to resolve organizational problems. Like the scientific method you used in high school science, the problem solving process applies to a problem, not a product. It is very much as applicable to the service end of the organization as it is to the manufacturing floor.

Excuse 2: We Tried That and It Did Not Work

The literature is loaded with examples of organizations, which tried to make a change and were unsuccessful. There is a myriad of reasons behind these failures, which are discussed as follows:

Exercise 4.2   We Tried That

Think about your organization for a moment and consider the last time your organization tried to make a change and it failed. Think out of the box and write down why it failed.

_____

_____

_____

_____

There are many reasons why these change efforts fail. First, the human capital assets were not behind the change effort. They were not shown why the change was necessary. They were not shown the various alternative outcomes (what will my job look like if we make the change vs. what will my job look like if we do nothing). Second, management gave lip service to the change effort. If upper management is not totally in favor of the change effort they will knowingly or unknowingly set up stumbling blocks to the process. In order for you to successfully implement the new culture, management must walk the walk and talk the talk. They must demonstrate that they are all for the effort you are undertaking.

While I am talking about management involvement, there is a flip side to this coin. This occurs when a long-time serving manager (s) makes the conscious decision to sabotage the process of change. They might not do it openly, but they do create obstacles to successful change. In meetings, they very well might pretend to support the initiative, but behind the seasons they tell anyone who will listen that they have seen these efforts tried in the past and they never work. They tell their fellow workers that things have worked well here for years and there is no valid reason for the change.

Excuse 3: It Is Too Complex for Most Organizations

Exercise 4.3   Too Complex

Why did you believe that the process to change the way your organization would be too complex for the organization? What demands does the change process put on you that is beyond your capabilities to conduct the change efficiently?

_____

_____

_____

_____

The literature abounds with descriptions of the change process being highly centered on high-level analytical skills and working with numbers and statistics. It has recently come to my attention that Motorola had stopped training Black Belts because the human capital assets came to believe that it was too technical.

The use of the TLS Continuum in a wide variety of companies and industries has demonstrated that it does not necessarily have to be. As I stated in *Achieving HR Excellence through Six Sigma*, Jay Arthur of the firm KnowWare International clearly states that if you get a software program[*] which is properly constructed, all you have do is fill in the blanks and the software does the calculations for you. No need to be a mathematician. No need to understand statistics.

---

[*] There are three primary software packages on the market that will do what you need. First is QI Macros (KnowWare International http://qimacros.com); the second is Sigma XL (Sigma XL http://SigmaXL.com) and the third is Minitab (http://www.minitab.com/).

Excuse 4: That Is Just Not the Way We Do Things Around Here

Exercise 4.4 It Is Not the Way We Do Things

Think about your organization for a moment and consider the last time your organization tried to make a change and were told that it was not how we do things around here. Why did they say that you could not do it that way?

_____

_____

_____

_____

In Chapter 3, I discussed the reasoning behind the Ishikawa diagram and as well as in that discussion and here now in this discussion the Lean tool called "the 5 whys" comes into play. Let's walk through the typical scenario when you hear this excuse as to why something cannot be done.

The odds are pretty good that if you really look at the process in question, the history might go as follows.

Manager: We can't do that, it is just not the way we do things here.
Employee: Why not?
Manager: Because that is the way we have always done it.
Employee: But why?
Manager: Because management tells us that is the way we have to do it.
Employee: Why?
Manager: Because John Smith introduced the process years ago.
Employee: Why?
Manager: He attended a conference and heard about this great new way of doing things and brought it back to the company and introduced it.
Employee: Why?
Manager: I don't know.

Many times what we do as organizations, in reality has no basis for what might be good for the corporation in today's climate. It finds its basis in a member of management observing something in another organization or at a seminar and thinking it would work well in yours. That may not be totally correct and once it is embedded into the corporate DNA it becomes really difficult to remove it.

Chapter 4 has been all about the problems with change. As human beings, we tend to resist change and usually do so with the wide variety of excuses why something won't work. The basis for these arguments tend to have their bases in illogical reasoning, which can be turned around with the proper communication to all parties involved. We need to show them that while we understand their reluctance to change what they have done for an extended period of time, the changes we are recommending are required for the organization to sustain itself now and into the future. At the same time, we need to establish that if circumstances present, we may have to change our practices down the road once again.

Chapter 5

Where Oh Where Is the End of This Journey?

Ladies and gentlemen, as we start our descent, please make sure your seat backs and tray tables are in their full upright position. Make sure your seat belt is securely fastened and be sure that all carry-on luggage is stowed underneath the seat in front of you or in the overhead bins. Please turn off all electronic devices until we are safely parked at the gate. Thank you.

There is a short answer to where the end of the journey is. That answer is that the journey never ends. The larger answer requires a more in-depth look at the remainder of the journey.

In the preface, I charged you with undertaking a unique journey. I suggested that this journey began with a very clear departure point centered on the problem(s) that faced the organization. While the journey has no definable final destination, it does generate two key performance indicators (KPIs) going forward.

The KPI is that once you begin this journey there is no going back to the old business environment. This is due to the fact that the business environment from which you left no longer exists. The way your organization functions has fundamentally changed. It is no longer content with the way we have always done things. In part, this is due to a new vision or corporate culture that has come out of your improvement efforts.

The second KPI is that the journey has created a new normal for the organization. This new normal is characterized by a renewed vision for the future of the organization. The new normal is a layover unlike the one discussed in Chapter 4. Unlike the earlier layover, this one is not caused by resistance to change within the organization. This layover is due to resolving one issue only to uncover a new problem area. The layover represents the point in time between the two projects. The new normal represents a closed cycle, which is continuously returning to the beginning of the process as we complete another improvement cycle.

Chapter 5 takes us through the last two stages of the Define–Measure–Analyze–Improve–Control (DMAIC) process. The chapters that preceded this point covered the first three steps of the DMAIC process. We began by identifying the parties to the processes within the workplace. These parties are our stakeholders who directly or indirectly contribute to the beginning of our processes. These parties became the crux of the suppliers, inputs, process, outputs, and customers (SIPOC) form, which we completed in Chapter 2. By identifying the components of the SIPOC and creating the process map, we were able to establish the current state of processes within the organization.

With the SIPOC and process maps in place we turn to the next part of the process, which is represented by the introduction of our customers' views of the world. The Voice of the Customer Matrix identifies for your organization what the customer is willing to pay for in delivering our product or service to them. From there I looked at the Ishikawa diagram to determine what were the causes of the gaps that appeared between the current state and what the customer demanded.

Based on the analysis of the differences between the customer demands and the current state we were able to create a Dettmer's Goal Tree to show where we go next.

The remainder of this chapter is devoted on how we get through both the improve and the control stages of the process along with how we implement the organizational change. Keep in mind that your goal is to create a new normal for the way the organization operates.

Basics of the New Culture

The creation of the new normal requires your organization to change its focus. It requires that the total organization structure be centered on the complete integration of strategy, innovation and alignment. As I stated in *Achieving HR Excellence through Six Sigma*, this innovation process is based on three interdependent pillars—customer centric, culture specific, and organizational alignment. The remainder of Chapter 5 will look at how to take these three pillars and implement them into the new corporate culture arising out of the creation of HR centers of excellence.

The creation of a seamless view of the organization is the guiding factor, which determines the success of the transformation process. If you are to fully comprehend the impact of the new cultural model we must delve deeper into the path to get there (Figure 5.1).

Dr. Tony Alessandra, in his book *The Platinum Rule,** suggests that the primary reason organizations exist is to acquire and maintain customers. If Tony is in fact correct, then part of the equation is the ability to hear the message that our internal and external customers are telling us.

On page 45, I discussed the use of the Voice of the Customer Matrix, which visually tells us what that message is. The message further informs the organization what the customer is willing to pay for to obtain our services or products.

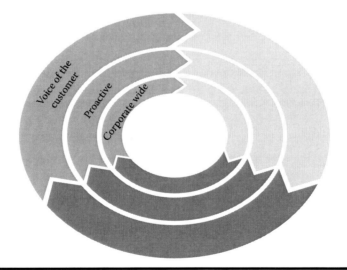

Figure 5.1   Voice of the customer element.

* OTE

Tactic 1: Move to a Proactive Stance within HR

Exercise 5.1   Reactive versus Proactive

Think about your organization as well as your functional area and determine whether you are putting out fires or performing the actions to remove the conditions that cause the fires in the first place.

_____

_____

_____

_____

I discussed earlier in this work and the original book that the path you take on this journey determines how successful you will be going forward. I suspect many of you are currently employed in a workplace which is reactive in nature. An employee files a complaint so HR jumps on the process to resolve the problem. A hiring manager tells you that he does not have adequate staffing so HR jumps on the bandwagon to resolve the issue. We continually play fireman to the corporate problems.

The new normal requires that we change that around and we need to become proactive to these issues. We need to assess why these situations arise and take steps to remove their occurrences ahead of the game. The other part of the move to proactive HR is that the effort to get away from firefighting is not unique to the HR department. As a result, this proactive stance must be embedded across the corporate organization and functions. From my perspective, there are three further actions that you can undertake which will embed the changed philosophy within your organization.

Tactic 2: Go and See

The only authentic way for you to understand what is going on in your organization is from being in the middle of it. Taiichi Ohno, the father of the Toyota Production System, used to tell his managers that you do not understand what is going on in your organization from your corner office.

He required his managers to spend time standing in a circle on the factory floor and observing what was going on. Exercise 5.2 will enable you to apply this concept to your own organization.

Exercise 5.2   Stand in the Circle

Think about the last time you left your office and consider what you observed. Were there processes that were blatantly problems or were there process steps that were just under the radar enough to be a problem?

_____

_____

_____

_____

When you thought about your responses to Exercise 5.2, did you discover something you had not thought of in the past? Let me help you get a better handle on how to view your organizational processes. Tracy Parks, the chief executive officer (CEO) of the consulting firm Simplicated, LLC, has developed an exercise based on Ohno's concept of standing in a circle to help you understand how things work in your organization.

In Exercise 5.3 follow her time limits and complete the exercise and the attached worksheet.

Exercise 5.3   Stand in the Circle Worksheet

Utilizing Simplicated's Stand in a Circle worksheet, can you identify the real problems in your organization?

_____

_____

_____

Stand in a Circle Exercise[*]

The exercise is called "Stand in a Circle" and is said to have originated with Taiichi Ohno, the father of the Toyota Production System (later known as Lean Manufacturing) in an effort to help managers understand and "see" waste.

Eighty percent of the purpose of this exercise is to build awareness and rewire your brain to *see* many small problems. Twenty percent of the process is purposed toward actual improvements. The more you are able to see the *"hard to see"* waste, the more you will be able to help your clients see the same.

Gather the following tools and read the following steps to get started:

- You will need to print a copy of the following Stand in a Circle worksheet
- Grab a pencil or pen and locate a clipboard or firm writing surface
- Put on comfortable shoes (you will be standing for 60 minutes)
- Set aside just over an hour of time
- A camera is preferred but optional[†]

Steps:

1. Choose a spot in *your* work environment.
2. For 30 minutes, stand and observe—silently.
3. The key is to practice what the Japanese call *kizuki*; the ability to notice.
4. Write down anything you notice that results in waste—energy, time, a safety concern, and abnormalities of any kind, maybe something that you notice you're not doing as efficiently as you could be.
5. Your task is to find 30 things—that's one every minute, including writing time!

Notes:

- Just observe and write—no need to comment or discuss with others (other than within necessity of being polite).
- Describe what you see and why you see this results in waste.
- Stay in *one* area and look deeply; it's easy to find 30 things if you flutter around like a butterfly and point out the large obvious wastes—instead, plant yourself like a tree and really see.

---

[*] The exercise is used with permission of Simplicated, LLC (http://www.simplicated.com).
[†] Alessandra, Tony, and Michael J. O'Connor. *The Platinum Rule.* New York, NY: Warner Books, 1996.

■ Sometimes waste can be hard to spot—if you need a place to begin, look for issues pertaining to safety, quality, environment, or energy losses. Do lights need to be turned off? Perhaps you need better lighting? Is there a counter, carpet, wall, file cabinet, desk area, or storage area in need of cleaning? Any work positions with bad ergonomics, awkward access?

That's half of the exercise; now take another 30 minutes to

1. Choose *one* of the items you noted and make some type of improvement.
2. Create a next action for another of your notations.

	Stand in a Circle Exercise Worksheet		Costing You			
	Observation	**Waste Category**	**Space**	**Time**	**Energy**	**Money**
1						
2						
3						
4						
5						
6						
7						
8						
9						
10						
11						
12						
13						
14						
15						
16						

(Continued)

	Stand in a Circle Exercise Worksheet		Costing You			
	Observation	**Waste Category**	**Space**	**Time**	**Energy**	**Money**
17						
18						
19						
20						
21						
22						
23						
24						
25						
26						
27						
28						
29						
30						

Name: Date:

	Use this list of categories or create your own.					
1	Ergonomic issue					
2	Potential safety hazard					
3	Energy inefficiencies					
4	Environmental distraction					

(Continued)

	Use this list of categories or create your own.					
5	Cleanliness and aesthetics issue					
6	Taking too long to find what is needed					
7	Too many steps to get to what is needed					
8	Too hard to access (reaching/ unloading/loading)					
9	More quantity of (X) than needed to keep/store					
10	Excess or clutter					
11	Not enough space, storage, shelving					
12	Walking around things to access other things					
13	Running out of supplies without warning					
14	Stuff not needed in this space					
15	Obsolete items					
16	Out-of-date items					
17	Nonfunctioning items					
18	Broken items					

(Continued)

	Use this list of categories or create your own.					
19	Takes too long to process or complete					
20	Too many steps to finish what has to get done					
21	Overly complex processes					
22	Not getting a process right every time					
23	Not having a clearly defined process for (X)					
24	Backlog					
25	Logjams					
26	Backsliding/letting systems deteriorate					
27	Planning issues					
28	No clarity around a progress area					
29	Poor follow-through					
30	Lack of execution					

The Ohno Stand in a Circle tool is primarily to be used for looking at the demands of internal customers. However, I have already discussed that you also have external customers. To understand this segment of your business we need a way to apply the concept of Standing in the Circle to this other aspect of your business. Like your internal organization, the external segment of the supply chain may also have its obstacles to your process. This can be achieved through a series of field visits to the customer base. Exercise 5.4 will take you on that journey.

Exercise 5.4   Field Visit

You are out in the field with your leading business development person, visiting customers. What information would assist you in meeting the voice of the customer from an HR perspective?

_____

_____

_____

_____

Earlier I asked you to lay out the steps in your hiring process in the form of a process map. One of the first blocks more than likely was the creation of a job requisition and or a job description. One of the easiest methods of determining the content of either of those documents is to ask your external customers. If you are like a majority of human resources professionals, I have just suggested a concept totally foreign to your business perspective. I would suggest that you spend 1 day a month out in the field with your best business development person. Your role in the field visits is to ask the customer for some assistance in the form of outlining what characteristics the customer finds beneficial to them in dealing with your organization.

Consider this scenario:

HR Representative: I greatly appreciate you giving us time to visit with you today. If you don't mind, I have a couple of questions I would like to discuss with you?

Client—How can I be of help?

HR Representative—We value your business and need your input. When your staff interacts with our customer service representatives (or whoever they interact with) what attributes do you expect to enhance your experiences in working with our staff?

We asked the client what are the characteristics of the ideal employee with whom they had to interact. The response to your questions provides you with the basis for the construction of both your job descriptions and the job requisitions. It provides you with a list of the key performance indicators for your specific positions. It in essence provides you with a picture of just what the customer is willing to pay you for.

Another aspect of the go-and-see effort is to look at the flow of information and people through the organization (Figure 5.2).

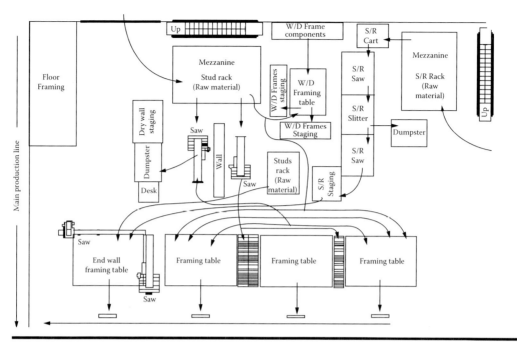

Figure 5.2 Spaghetti diagram.

Exercise 5.5 Organizational Flow

As you are out of your office looking at how things flow through the organization, did you observe anything that looked like it took an extraordinary amount of time to complete? If so, why?

_____

_____

_____

_____

We can do this by utilizing the tool we call a spaghetti diagram. It maps out the flow through the organization. The preceding spaghetti diagram is a process map of the flow of people and data through the organization. When done properly, it clearly manifests the errors in the way things are done. A well-known financial services company used this tool to follow a loan application for a new home purchase. When the process was done that application had moved the distance of eight miles* from beginning to end. Each step of the process is connected to the next step by a series of lines and arrows. If the process is working properly, there should be a minimal number of arrows connecting to each other. If you are out of sync with the rest of the process, you end up with a visual picture that looks much like a bowl of spaghetti. When you have finished the spaghetti diagram, your next task is to look at it with open eyes and see where certain steps can be eliminated to allow the process to be faster, cheaper, and better.

Tactic 3: Focus on the Process

Exercise 5.6   Process or People

> Stop and think for a moment. Your hiring manager comes to you and tells you that the new employee is not working out and we have to get rid of him. You work in an employment-at-will state, but is that really the best answer? How would you respond to the hiring manager?

I fully understand that we are human. When faced with obstacles or adversity the first tendency is to identify whom we can blame for the situation. As managers, we tend to immediately decide that when an organization has a problem, it has to be a people problem.

This is not to say that there are not detractors within the organization who are dead set against the changes we are implementing. They are the ones exemplified by the discussion in Chapter 4. But this comes from the resistance to change and not the organization as a whole.

In order to achieve a customer-centric view, it is necessary for us to change our focus so that the very first place we look when a problem arises is the process itself. In many, if not in all of these situations, it is the process and the way we delivery it that is creating the problems. We have constructed steps,

---

* The description of this project was provided by one of the attendees in our 2-day Achieving HR Excellence through Six Sigma class.

which made sense at the time of creation, but as time passed on we did not review them to see if the steps made the same sense as when they were created.

Tactic 4: Do It Now

Exercise 5.7   When If Not Now?

When your organization last decided to make a change in the way it did things, how long did it take for management to decide to make the change happen?

_____

_____

_____

_____

It is critical we recognize that the decisions to correct processes must be done quickly. Part of the trio of goals in the process improvement spectrum is do things faster. The experiences discussed in *Achieving HR Excellence through Six Sigma* regarding the GE Workout* and the Change Acceleration Process highlight the need for these actions.

There is a disadvantage to the voice of the customer in that more often than not we listen to the voice of the customer post that a problem exists. The customer has expressed some dissatisfaction with our services or products and so we retroactively respond. The purpose of Exercise 5.3 is to begin the process of asking questions before we have a problem.

Tactic 5: Gain Knowledge

I have previously discussed that our workplaces are changing rapidly. Some of the changes are caused by the introduction of new services and products. Others are caused by the ever-changing world in which we reside. Nevertheless, we need to learn what is working and what is not working. An additional Six Sigma methodology tool available to you to gain that crucial need which is crucial to your success is benchmarking.

---

* For a more in-depth understanding of the GE Workout Process, look at Dave Ulrich's book on the topic, *GE Workout* (New York, NY: McGraw Hill, 2002).

Exercise 5.8   Where Would I Go?

Your CEO has asked you to find out what the best practices are to resolve a particular issue. What sources would you utilize to find the answers to the CEO's question?

_____

_____

_____

_____

Human resource professionals for years have utilized the benchmarking tool in the delivery of their services to the organization. We have benchmarked the programs other companies our size have used to offer benefits. We have used benchmarking when determining whether our salary packages are aligned with the rest of the industry.

Using these same processes we can review how other organizations have undertaken the solution of similar problems to ours and what worked and what did not. *Achieving HR Excellence through Six Sigma* contained case studies from Ceridian, BGI, and others to demonstrate where organizations had utilized the skills discussed previously in this book.

Tactic 6: Corporate Mantra

Exercise 5.9   Who Is Listening?

You are the vice president of HR and you have just implemented a new policy and procedure in alignment with the latest benchmarking of HR practices. Who is listening to your effort?

_____

_____

_____

_____

None of what I have discussed so far is worth the effort if no one listens. The final tool in the customer-centric pillar is that this change must become the corporate mantra. For it to become the corporate mantra, it has to become embedded in everything the organization does. The mantra is part of our corporate brand. It is part of our mission statement. It is part of our corporate values. It is part of our image delivered to the marketplace. It has to be the tacit understanding that this is the way we do business because our customers demand that we do it this way. If someone can't work within the new environment then they either need to get trained or coached on how to leave the organization.

Organizational Alignment

Every organization, either in writing or implied, has a mission, a vision, or an operating statement, which delineates their corporate culture. Your corporate culture tells the world who you are and what you stand for. The combination of the corporate culture and the voice of the customer are the keys to your organizational alignment. This combination, however, is unique to your organization. You can't go down the street to your competitor and find the exact same cultural components. The corporate culture is so unique that benchmarking, which I discussed earlier, will be of limited value. We need to begin by establishing a clear view of just what our organizational culture is and the role it plays within your organization. Your organization can do that by implementing the following seven strategy tools.

Tactic 7: Change Managers to Leaders

Exercise 5.10 Corporate Governance

How is your organization governed? What is the anticipation of the role of your human capital assets within the organization?

_____

_____

_____

_____

Go to Amazon and search for the term "management books." Amazon states that there are 139,300 titles available in that subject area. The vast majority of them will advocate the command and control manager style of operating. Management decides that something will be done and hands down an edict, which tells the organization hierarchy, "This is the way it will be done."

In the Theory of Constraints–Lean–Six Sigma (TLS) Continuum, we require a new approach to this long-standing view of the organization. Our managers need to migrate to a new philosophy. It is one founded in the belief of the individual human capital assets. You no longer "manage" a segment of the organization but rather you are part of the whole system model. As leaders, we have new goals. We need to strive to improve the work environment for all of our human capital assets, much like the Quaker Business Model.* Our goal is for an employer to seek for others, the best life of which they are capable. Our view of the world is not confined to our silo but must include the whole system we call work.

The success of the TLS continuum is based on the view that an organization only functions at its optimum when everyone is involved in the final consensus on the optimal solution.

---

* More information on the Quaker Business Model can be found at http://qandb.org/resources /publications/85-resources/publications/165-quakers-a-business-group-business-principles.

Tactic 8: Transformational Leaders

Is there a difference between a leader and a transformational leader? The response to the question is centered on your outlook of what your job responsibilities are. If you believe that your role is to come to work and manage people, then you do not understand your new role.

On the other hand, if you come to work and are taking positive steps toward the implementation of empowered change in your organization, then you meet the criteria for being a transformational leader.

Exercise 5.11   Leadership Role

As a leader, what is your role within the organization?

_____

_____

_____

_____

There is a clear difference between the manager turned leader as we discussed in the previous strategy tool and the transformational leader. The transformational leader looks at the organization with a different, unique eye. This unique eye is focused on the opportunities within the organization where they can empower change. When they have discovered these opportunities they then assume the responsibility to lead that change. They must create a road map for that change much like I have done in this book and they must ensure that everyone is on the same page going forward. I am not suggesting that this new transformational leader is a lone wolf, although he or she may start out that way. Whatever change they are guiding must be in total alignment with the leadership vision for the organization. The changes they are leading are changing not a single process but the way the total organization functions—the way the total organization operates. It is creating a new vision, a new mission, and a new work environment. You are taking the organization from where it is to a place it has never been.

Tactic 9: Educate and Train

Exercise 5.12   Educate versus Train

Organizations spend millions of dollars on training for their employees, but what is the difference to you between "educate" and "train"?

_____

_____

_____

_____

The TLS Continuum mandates that we need to follow a very clear path. We begin with the process of *educating* our organization about the new process. This education process explains what it is we are going to do, why we are going to do it, and how we are going to do it. There is one final piece of the educate side of the equation and that is that we need to educate the organization regarding what the consequences are if we do nothing and remain in a state of status quo.

Once we educate the organization, we assume a new role. In any organization there will be individuals who either can't or won't obtain the necessary skills to perform the duties we ask them to do. In these cases, we need to immediately determine which option we are dealing with. The major reason in most cases is that the individual either did not receive or understand the directions they were given. In this case, the transformational leader must *train* the individual to get them up to the key performance indicator level required. If at first we are not successful, then we need to continue to train the individual until they get the required skills. There also may be a point at which the employee reaches a level that is better than it was but still does not meet the required skills, and at the point we reverse the cycle and *educate* them about alternatives available for them.

For those who absolutely refuse to become involved with the new processes, the only thing that can be done is to educate them about what options are available outside the organization.

Tactic 10: Break Down Silos

Exercise 5.13 Silos

Is your organization totally aligned, or do you still have
departments that think they are above the rest of the
organization?

_____

_____

_____

_____

Every organization has its departmental functions, and that is a fact
of corporate life. What is not true is that they have to operate in this
self-ordained vacuum compared with the rest of the organization. While
some silos such as IT may be needed, they must function within the total
organizational alignment plan. This is why the benefits of cross-functional
teams are so important in the TLS Continuum.

Tactic 11: Avoid Quotas

Deming told us that the existence of quotas was demeaning to the
organization. In many cases, these quotas are based on data that was pulled
out of thin air. Forget the arbitrary number and look at the HR metrics that
mean something to the organization. For example, it is of more benefit to
the organization to understand when a department is most likely to lose a
key employee rather than that we need to hire X number of employees per
month to meet our talent needs.

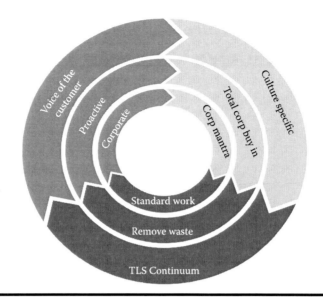

Figure 5.3   Corporate culture specific.

Tactic 12: Coach

Think about the situation I talked about earlier regarding educate and train. The TLS Continuum places on each manager a critical role. It is your responsibility to provide the environment in which each and every human capital asset is allowed to develop to their maximum potential. The manager's role in this scenario is to take the individual from where they are and guide them to the point where they meet the potential. Sometimes the manager will suggest that there is a different role in the organization; other times the path for that individual is to be allowed to graciously exit the organization (Figure 5.3).

The TLS Continuum—Optimal Organization Empowerment

The final pillar in the TLS continuum is the optimization of the change effort. This is the segment where the organization ensures that your efforts to empower organization change have gained traction for the long term. The final pillar represents the control stage of the DMAIC process. This phase contains the final four strategic tools that are presented in this book.

Tactic 13: Long-Term Planning to Optimize Services

Exercise 5.14   Succession Plan

Does your organization have a formalized succession plan in place? If a key member of this project is removed for whatever reasons, do you have someone who can seamlessly slide into his or her place?

_____

_____

_____

_____

Don't be alarmed if your answer to the questions in Exercise 5.14 was no. The majority of organizations do not have a succession plan in place. However, for the long-range success of any empowerment effort you must create a plan to ensure that the flow continues in the event of a departure, no matter what the cause. It further ties into how well your processes are working.

Part of optimal organizational empowerment is based in the creation of a specific standard of work for each process within the organization. The total organization needs to understand that if a process is begun, it is completed using the same steps each and every time. We have in essence created a standard of work that becomes the benchmark as to how we are doing as an organization. We may have multiple standards of work governing the organization with the key being it is a process we follow each and every time we utilize that process.

Tactic 14: Always a Better Way

We stressed in the beginning of this book that you were embarking on a journey which had no ending. The reason for this statement is that there is no finite way to resolve the issue you have uncovered in this journey. When you have total organizational involvement, the corporate subject matter experts (the frontline employees) will know when there is a better way to do something. The way they resolve the problem may be totally different than your organization has ever done it before. You need to maintain an open mind to the new suggestions for improving your processes.

Tactic 15: Poka Yoke

Another vital part of this final leg of the current journey is to remove variation from the process. These variations to the process are nonvalue added activities to the customer and to the organization. Chapter 5 in *Achieving HR Excellence through Six Sigma* outlined in detail the nine kinds of nonvalue added activities. The important take away here is that to complete the control state and the optimal organization empowerment we need to ensure that the standard of work eliminates the chance for error. Much like the automotive shop where there is a pegboard with outlines of where the tools go, the human resources function needs to design a system in which everything has its place so that the entire organization knows how to place the process into action.

Tactic 16: Drive Out Fear

Exercise 5.15 Driving Out Fear

Is your organization open to experimentation on the part of your human capital assets, or are they penalized in the end-of-the-year performance reviews?

_____

_____

_____

_____

I suggested in the beginning of *Achieving HR Excellence through Six Sigma* that as HR professionals you had a decision to make. That decision entailed deciding whether you truly wanted to continue in an HR role. It is our belief that in order for you to continue, you need to speak the language of business. More important, you must understand that, much like your high school science classes and the scientific method, the DMAIC process provides you with a systematic way to test your hypothesis as to the solutions to your problems. Like the scientific method, we enter the measure stage with the intent to test our expected solutions to the problem. Like the scientific method, some solutions will succeed and some will fail.

The point here is not that it happens but rather we can't expect that our efforts to empower organizational change will be necessarily a smooth ride. When things go wrong, and they will, we can't hold those who worked on the process improvement to be responsible because something did not work. The major corporations who have been successful at this effort know that. They understand that something in the process is why it did not work. They additionally realize that, like our scientific method example mentioned earlier, we do not hold the failure as a stick over the human capital asset's heads at performance time.

As we stated in the first book, change is frightful. Change is scary. Change is about developing a problem-solving method that works for your organization. Change is about taking the risk that your suggestions may be in error. As Deming suggested, we must change the organization to empower change without retribution. We need to ensure that no human capital asset within the organization is afraid to make a mistake.

The human capital assets need to know and understand this. Equally management needs to know and understand this.

Chapter 6

This Is Where I Get Off

I have a goal in my professional life to deliver a message. It is a message that will transform our business world to greater heights. If we go back to the time of the emancipation proclamation, we were deeply involved in the agricultural age. This was a period when the family ran the farm and each individual had an integral part in the success of the farm. As we moved to the industrial age, we lost that human capital asset focus.

In a sense, we have come to this point in our business development to cash a check. Starting with the Quaker business model, business laid out a promise to the organization that we, as management, would take care of our most valued tool in our arsenal to compete in the global marketplace— our human capital assets that are now nonowned, leased corporate assets. This promise stated that all programs initiated by the organization would be centered on a guarantee of being a valued part of the organization. As we look at many organizations today, it increasingly obvious that American business has defaulted on this promise. The focus moved from considering the human capital asset as such to being an expense item that affected the corporate bottom line.

But we refuse to believe that the promise is bankrupt. We refuse to believe that there is no room for the organizations to change in the global workplace. This means, as Dr. Deming suggested, we need to move to a new philosophy in which management learns their responsibilities and takes on leadership for change.

If you are reading this page, you are here for one of two reasons. First, there is a percentage of you who will read the introduction and the end of a book to get a feel for the contents of the book. If that is your reason for being here, you have missed a lot. You have missed the acquisition of the basic knowledge of why we need change and how to work with the tools in the TLS Continuum to achieve that change.

The second reason you are here is because you have participated in this journey since its inception and we thank you for being receptive to our message.

While the TLS (Theory of Constraints–Lean–Six Sigma) Continuum journey is fret with "alligators," it is an exciting journey and we were privileged to have you join us. There is an old English adage dating back to 1175 that states that you can lead a horse to water but you can't make it drink. It in essence is where we are now in the journey to process improvement.

It has been my honor to guide you this point. I have taken this opportunity to lay out my message about the road map to enable you to gain the resources to empower your organizational change. I can do no more and no less. I am the carrier of a critical message for sustainability of your organization and for you as a professional. Hopefully, I have presented the importance of taking the journey with all its pitfalls and successes. The intent was to provide you with a new set of glasses from which you viewed the world, your organization, and how you serve your customers, both external and internal. The intent of this work was for you to gain the perspective that those attending the 2-day seminar have. They have come away with the belief that they never thought of viewing the human resources (HR) function in the way they do now.

I have done all I can to be your teacher and your sensei on how to begin this journey. There is nothing more that I can contribute to the success of your personal journey.

From here on out, it is your journey and your choice as to whether you carry it further. It is your choice whether you gain the knowledge and understanding of your internal and external customers. It is your choice whether you transfer that knowledge to ensuring that you only deliver what they are prepared to pay you for. It is your choice whether you can ascertain the roles that your customers, vendors, and management play in the error-free delivery of your services and products to those customers when they need them, where they need them and how they need them. You decide whether you are truly delivering your services faster, better, and cheaper than the next person.

You have a choice to make. Do you play it safe and continue in the mediocre, commodity-based path that the vast majority of HR people follow in, or do you take the risk and strive for a whole new vision of where your organization can go and do.

Are you willing to eliminate or at best reduce the fear of making a mistake and go for it and empower that change required for your organization to thrive in this rapidly changing global workplace we are in today?

I need to also remind the reader that since you began this journey, your old comfort zone most likely no longer exists in the format you remember it. This leaves you with the options of continuing the journey or failing to provide the valuable human capital management perspective that your organization needs to survive.

The TLS Continuum provides you with the road map to get to that new place where you have never been. The TLS Continuum provides you with the tools and procedures to ease the journey to this new culture. This new philosophy, which runs rampant through the entire organization, determines how you precede going forward. The only way this will succeed is if the entire organization understands what is in it for them, what is not in it for them if we don't take the action, and what the path to this new normal is.

Once again I thank you for joining me on this journey. The only thing we ask in return is that you take the chance and begin the journey not with me or with a class of students but with a self-review of your own situation. If you do so, you will become a better part of the organization. As HR professionals you are the catalyst for the empowerment to change due to your responsibility for the management of the human capital assets. Embrace that power. Embrace the new function you will play.

I leave you with one expectation. Each and every one of you who has read this book will go forward and be focused, flexible, and fast within your organizations. My hope is that you will embrace these opportunities to improve the processes that in turn will grow your organization— that you will embrace these opportunities to empower change within your organization, leading to a new normal embedded throughout the organization and centered on the TLS Continuum spectrum.

There is one more thing we ask in return for my guidance along this journey. Pay it forward. Share the message with your peers both inside and outside your organization. Become the additional messenger to alert your fellow professionals to the dynamic opportunities that you have discovered in the course of the journey. Learn how to deliver your message in the strongest way possible. Reach out in a method where you will be heard. You have seen the light of the future and now have the task to show others the light. I have refrained from recommending one resource over another but in learning how to deliver your version of my message I would highly suggest you obtain a copy of Sally Hogshead's *How the World Sees You.** It will change the way you deliver the message in a dramatic way.

I look forward to hearing about your successes.

---

* Hogshead, Sally. *How the World Sees You.* New York, NY: Harper Business, 2014.

Chapter 7

Case Studies

The purpose of this *Field Guide to Achieving HR Excellence through Six Sigma* was to provide you with the tools that will enable you to empower change within your organization. In Chapter 5, we discussed a tool out of the toolbox called benchmarking.

Benchmarking is a tool that many human resource professionals are familiar with, as we have used it for years. You are writing a new policy so you reach out to the HR community to see what others have included in their similar policies. You are considering a revision to your compensation plan, so you reach out to the global marketplace to see how others are paying professionals with similar skills and education. These are all examples of benchmarking. It should be noted here that the results from benchmarking can have either a positive or negative effect on your organization.

In trying to bring this road map to a natural conclusion, I wanted to find a way to demonstrate through benchmarking what others have done along the way toward implementing the TLS Continuum road map. At the same time, my goal is to present to you the reader evidence-based information that would explain the process improvement path so that no matter what your learning style you would be able to draw the same conclusions from the projects presented in Chapter 7.

The Merriam-Webster dictionary defines a case study as a published report about a person, group, or situation that has been studied over time or a situation in real life that can be looked at or studied to learn about something. Those of you who have had experience studying case studies know that they typically come in the form of a multiple-page document, which in narrative form presents the critical information regarding the events under consideration. They provide a clear picture of processes within organizations. So, I could not think of a better way to complete this chapter than to provide you with several case studies of organizations that have used the tools we have discussed.

Having said that, I will be creating case studies with a twist. These case studies will have a limited amount of narrative. This is done on purpose to respond to the learning styles of the reader. In each case study that follows, I will provide you with a narrative pertaining to two aspects of the situation involved. First, I will provide you with a brief paragraph describing the organization involved. Second, I will provide you with a brief paragraph describing the problem that was being presented. The remainder of the case study will be all the actual project documents that the organization used. One last caveat is needed here. In each case, these are real projects with real results, which generated positive results for the organizations involved. Finally, we will include a conclusion section, which will describe the results of the project.

Following are five case studies each of which used the DMAIC process to respond to an organizational real problem.

The first case study, titled "Training Effectiveness: Is the Cost Justified?" was the author's Black Belt project. It looked at the worldwide efforts to evaluate training and whether the results made the cost we spend (according to *Workforce* magazine in 2008, corporations spent $56.2 billion on training) for training justifiable to an organization.

The second case study is from Sparton Electronics and deals with the effective time to hire new employees. This project was submitted as the requirements to complete our *How to Become the Critical HR Leader You Are Meant to Be* seminar.

The remaining three case studies come from a medical device manufacturing corporation dealing with both service and manufacturing examples of process applications.

List of Case Studies

  Case Study 1

    Organization: Daniel Bloom & Associates, Inc. (DBAI)

    Problem: Training effectiveness: Is the cost justified?

Case Study 2
  Organization: Sparton Electronics
  Problem: Excessive hiring time

Case Study 3
  Organization: Electromechanical Medical Device Manufacturer
  Problem: Extended hiring time

Case Study 4
  Organization: Electromechanical Medical Device Manufacturer
  Problem: Reduction of hold time on invoices

Case Study 5
  Organization: Electromechanical Medical Device Manufacturer
  Problem: Process of work packet failure to follow standard of work

Case Study 1: Training Effectiveness: Is the Cost Justified?

The Organization: Created in 1980 and incorporated as a Florida corporation in 1988, DBAI is a boutique HR consulting firm specializing in providing services in the areas of HR strategy, the application of the Six Sigma methodology to HR, retained HR, coaching, and training. In addition, we facilitate presentations for associations across a wide spectrum of industries on HR matters. Based in West Central Florida, we service our clients as subject matter experts in the field of corporate mobility. We are HR strategists assisting organizations to empower change within their organizations, and our client base ranges from the Fortune 100 to small and medium enterprises nationwide.

The Project: The business environment began as agricultural based, and, as we began the move to the cities, the marketplace fundamentally changed. In the Industrial Age, we needed to discover ways to be competitive with other firms doing the same thing we were doing. This was based on becoming more innovative in the way we developed products. The essence of this was the human capital investment that businesses undertook. The problem was that the human capital aspect in the Industrial Age was considered to be an expense of the organization. As a result, when hard times arose in the marketplace, much like we saw in the global arena in 2009, the first thing organizations sought to do was to cut expenses through a reduction-in-force (RIF). As the world changed further, we moved from the value of the enterprise being based on what we made to an organization based on what we knew. This change fundamentally changed the way the human capital factor was viewed within the business. Our FTEs were now an asset, a nonowned asset, rather than an expense. With this change, the need was created to find a way to increasingly engage the FTEs within the organization. As the new generations entered the workforce, the developing career portfolio increasingly became an issue for recruitment and retention. Despite this new focus, training has always been one of the first areas for corporations to cut when times got bad.

On January 27, 2009, Daniel T. Bloom, the Six Sigma Black Belt on this project, with the approval of William Mazurek, project sponsor, began the process to determine whether the $56.2 billion expended was in fact a cost-effective use of corporate funds. The Black Belt Project stated that the current environment for training, in most cases, only involved an attempt to ascertain whether the FTEs that were being trained enjoyed the training. There was no attempt to discover whether the organization was achieving a return on their investment. The purpose of this report is to present the results of the evaluation of existing training program across multiple industry segments and explain the solutions being recommended to gain a better picture of the impact of training on the organization.

This project analysis utilized a detailed explanation of the current state of the industry, the available results of training evaluations, and the Six Sigma DMAIC methodology from which the participants were able to reach clear and demonstrable conclusions on whether corporate training is cost-effective both strategically and financially (Figures 7.1 through 7.5).

Figures

7.1. Project charter
7.2. SIPOC
7.3. Fishbone diagram
7.4. Balanced scorecard
7.5. Corporate metrics

Project Charter

Project Name / Title: Training Effectiveness: Are Our Training Programs Cost-Effective?	
Sponsoring Organization: Daniel Bloom and Associates, Inc.	
Project Sponsor: William F. Mazurek Six Sigma Black Belt	
Team Members (Name)	**Role**
Daniel T. Bloom	Black Belt Consultant
Tiffany Krueger First American Title	Training Provider
Pat Smolen PSCU Financial Services	Training Provider
Kevin Weafer KLA-Tencor	Training Provider
David Castaneda Lazy Days RV Superstore	Training Provider
Ed Nolen AAASouth	Training Provider
Principal Stakeholder	**Proposed Benefit**
Senior Management	More Engaged FTE's which will in turn make the business enterprise more productive
Training Providers	
Corporate Clients	
Corporate Employees (FTE's)	
Sponsor Approval Signature / Date:	

Preliminary Plan (Milestones)		Target Date	Actual Date	Approvals
Determine the scope of the project		01/27/2009		
Prepare and submit project charter		02/04/2009		
Determine evaluation methods		02/10/2009		
Analyze the training data		04/15/2009		
Construct dashboards		04/22/2009		
Construct Balance Scorecard		04/27/2009		
Deliver final product to stakeholders		05/06/2009		

Figure 7.1 DBAI project charter.   (*Continued*)

Project Name/Title:
Training Effectiveness: Are Our Training Programs Cost Effective?

Problem/Opportunity Statement

In today's competitive talent market, one attribute most sought after by the generation coming into the marketplace is the ability to enhance their career portfolio. The question for training providers and senior management is whether the training they provide is the right type (training versus education) to meet their needs. In order to determine this, we must investigate the availability of the correct tools to properly calculate our return on investment of the various training being delivered.

Project Goal: Solution/Recommendation

The goal of this project will be to create a visual dashboard which will enable the trainer provider to quickly determine from analyzing the selected evaluation methods how they are doing with the training programs and from there calculate the return on investment of said programs. After selecting the best venue for the evaluation, the strategies from that training will be embedded into a Kaplan and Norton Balanced Scorecard vehicle for future training development.

Resources Requested (What you need, $, personnel, time, etc.)
- Access to Corporate Training Program Statistics
- Data from the Kirkpatrick's Four Levels of Training Evaluation
- Data from the Phillips' Five Level ROI Model
- Data from Total Cost of Ownership calculations
- Data from DuPont Training Attribute Model
- Simple Training ROI

Project Impact Statement

Based on the selection of the evaluation methods of training, we should be able to demonstrate the best practices in designing training programs for the corporation which will enhance the career portfolios of the involved FTEs and at the same time, through increased employee engagement have a direct impact on the corporate bottom line by getting the most for the dollars spent in providing the training programs.

Figure 7.1   (*Continued*) DBAI project charter.

How to Use the Training Attribute Evaluation Tool—A User Guide

The Excel-based Training Attribute Evaluation Tool, developed out a Six Sigma Black Belt project, is a vehicle to provide management with a method to identify the relationship between the critical and quality aspects of the planned training to determine whether or not the organization is receiving a return on their training dollar investment. Below is a detailed explanation of the tool. Each worksheet of the tool is designed to carry the manager deeper into the training implication process.

SIPOC Diagram

Suppliers	Input	Process	Output	Customers
Performance development staff	Training need assessment	**Start:**	Increased efficiency	Corp human capital
Program developers	Management buy-in	Design of training programs	Increased engagement	Various corp departments
Program vendors	Stakeholder buy-in	Presentation of training programs		External customers
		Type of training (ILT, WBT, CBT)		
		High-Level Process Description:		
		END:		

Figure 7.2 DBAI SIPOC diagram. (*Continued*)

Suppliers	Input	Process	Output	Customers
		Training metrics		
		Calculation of training ROI		

Figure 7.2 (*Continued*) DBAI SIPOC diagram.

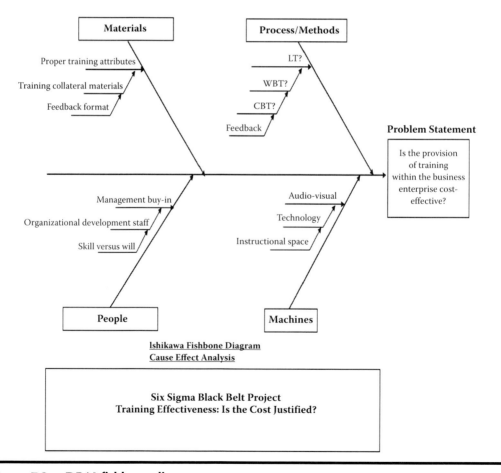

Figure 7.3 DBAI fishbone diagram.

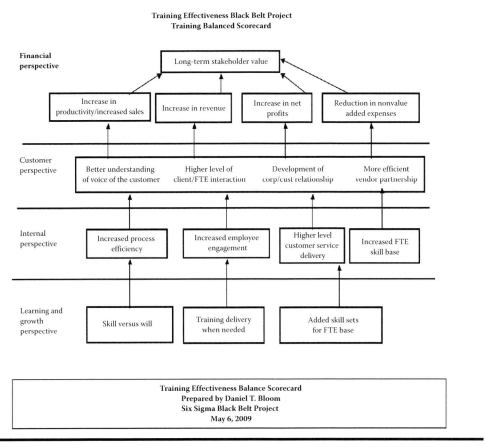

Training Effectiveness Black Belt Project
Training Balanced Scorecard

Figure 7.4   **DBAI balanced scorecard.**

Training Assessment Tool—Corporate Tactical Improvement Areas

The evaluation tool begins with the determination of those tactical areas that management feels are necessary to change in order to enhance the operations of the organization. While the list of tactical areas is organization specific, the following example provides a sample of the kinds of tactical improvement areas that might fit your organization. In the following examples, we have delineated 14 tactical areas that the example organization felt needed improvement. These tactical improvement areas constitute the basis of the rest of the tool worksheets.

In order to understand the tool in real terms, the 14 tactical improvement areas are defined as follows.

Corporate Metrics

Metric/corp	Corp 1	Corp 2	Corp 3	Corp 4	Corp 5	Corp 6
Annual sales volume	$24,000,000	$564,835,000	$2,521,716,000	$778,000,000	$8,195,605,000	$1,000,000,000
Total training hours		52,583	27,992	56,944	53,013	62,265
Total training—ITL		52,583	4,863	56,944	1,504	62,265
Total training—WBT			23,129		51,513	
Total training—CBT						
Total FTE trained		4,125	32,855	700	1,638	30,647
Total trained % revenue		0.001%	0.001%	0.0001%	0.00002%	0.003%
Total FTE—ITL						
Total FTE—WBT						
Total FTE—CBT						
Total cost of ownership						
Kirkpatrick reaction		4.7				

Figure 7.5   DBAI metrics.

- **Individual Performance Level**—Without exception business organizations through their management efforts have determined a certain level of productivity that is needed from each member of the organization. Deming has charged us with ridding the organizations of quotas, but these go beyond that. These individual performance levels are broken down into what each human capital asset must contribute to the organization in order for the overall organization to sustain itself.

- **Increased Peer Pressure (To Go Do a Good Job)**—One of the outcomes of the movement to a culture of quality is that it is everyone's responsibility to ensure that the organization is a place where defects are not tolerated. As a result, the second tactical area looks at the level of pressure placed on the human capital assets by their fellow workers to ensure that we meet the goal of quality work.

- **Employee Motivation (To Go the Extra Mile)**—In line with peer pressure, how far are our human capital assets willing to go to get the job done? Are we stuck in that's-not-my-job mind-sets? Do our human capital assets take ownership of the work with the goal of doing what is necessary to get it right the first time?

- **Meaningful Performance Assessment (Good/Better/Best)**—One of the difficulties in evaluating any training program is how to judge the ultimate outcomes of the training on corporate performance. Whether you use the Kilpatrick or the Phillips model, many trainers believe it is too difficult to evaluate these programs beyond a simple smile sheet. The manager is asked whether they believe that you have a meaningful way to determine the assessment model is good/better/best in class.

- **Incorporating Process Improvement as a Corporate Culture**—An organization can continuously conduct training programs for a wide variety of reasons. Sometimes we introduce training because the industry we are in requires it, such as for regulatory reasons. In other cases, training is conducted to improve the organization skill levels in the soft skill arena. In either case, the goal is to change the organizational culture. A key to the outcome is the support of upper management toward the new culture.

- **Achieving Bottom-Line Results**—Management understands that in order for the organization to survive, the organization must operate at a certain financial level. The belief of management is that by providing the training programs, the newly obtained skills will allow the organization to grow their revenues and as a result increase the bottom line of the organization.

■ **Respecting Our Corporate Values**—Organizations function as they do based on the organizational culture. One of the training expectations is that new and current employees will gain a better view and respect for those cultural aspects that run the organization.

■ **Increasing Our Competitive Advantage**—We are in an age where our human capital assets are corporate assets, based on the knowledge they have of both the industry and the organization they are functioning in. Training is expected to increase their value to the organization as a knowledge asset capable of bringing unique solutions for the customer base of the organization.

■ **Maximizing Employee Loyalty**—Much is said today about the lack of employee engagement. One key to changing this perspective is for the belief on the part of the human capital assets that they are a vital part of the organization.

■ **Employees Perceive Our Compensation Benefits to Be Fair**—Quality training has value. The goal of many of the human capital assets is to increase their career portfolio of applicable skills. Whether they are taking free training or a paid seminar, the human capital assets will understand that this is part of their compensation package. With this information, when they talk with their various networks, they will be in a position to evaluate whether they are receiving competitive benefits for the services they are providing to your organization.

■ **Building Trust through the Organization**—In order for training to be effective, it must cross all parts of the organization. Any training being offered to the organization should include not only line staff but also management. The purpose for the interaction between the levels is to develop the belief that each part of the organization has a valuable required role within the organization.

■ **Relationship Building (Between Levels, Across Levels)**—Look at many of your organizations in your industry and you will find that many of them have come to the realization that the path to high-performing organizations is through the use of high-performance teams. The purpose of the team is to all interact to resolve a critical issue within the organization. As the teams achieve their purpose, relationships are built across the organization with common goals.

■ **Networking within the Organization—Team-Building Benefits** A side benefit of the cross-functional team approach is that when team members look outside of their "silos," there may very well be talent resources within the organization that they never knew were there and available to the organization. In the process of utilizing the cross-functional teams, you learn where the resources are and how to utilize the resources for future projects.

■ **Open and Honest Coaching and Feedback**—The final tactical area is that of coaching and feedback. The Kirkpatrick model is the ability to be able to demonstrate that the training has improved the performance levels of the organization. Training should present a picture of where and how the human capital asset needs coaching to reach the next performance level.

Returning to the tool, we can now walk through the completion of the tool. Completion of the first worksheet within the training effectiveness evaluation tool (TREEAT) is based on the following tasks.

Task 1: We have identified the tactical improvement areas and so now it is the responsibility of management to begin the analysis of the organization based on these tactical areas. The first column in this worksheet asks you on a scale of 1–10, with 10 being superior, to assess where you are in each of the tactical areas. This analysis represents your current state as it pertains to each tactical area. If you look at the following example, in our sample organization the rating scales range from 2 to 6. Once the complete analysis is done it provides us the ability to identify the critical few tactical areas that need the most attention. If you look at the ratings example, the critical few most likely would be represented by employee motivation and meaningful performance assessment since they are both shown with a rating of "2."

Task 2: With management having identified the current state it now becomes critical that you take it the next step. This involves management determining what the future state would look like. Following the training being delivered, how do you picture the organization? Once again we use the same rating scale and rate each of these areas on the same 1–10 rating scale, with 10 being superior.

Task 3: The final task on this initial worksheet is to determine how important that tactical area is to the organization. Every organization has its priorities and the training outcomes are no different. Using the same 1–10 scale, management will rate each tactical area on the basis of how important is that area to the future of the organization.

The worksheet has embedded in it formulas which determine how to calculate an improvement goal based on the comparison of the current state, the future state, and the business priorities. This calculation is carried forward to a later worksheet (Figure 7.6).

Take a moment and review the discussion of Dettmer's Goal Tree*. Dettmer suggested that we begin with a goal (corporate tactical improvement areas) and from there we have to determine first in order for us to achieve the goal we need to have certain conditions to be present.

In this second worksheet, we have the goal and now need to identify those conditions necessary to achieve the intended training outcome. Below is a look at the goal versus condition required to achieve the

Corporate Tactical Improvement Areas for 2009	Current Performance (1–10)	Corporate Goal (1–10)	Business Priority (1–10)	Improvement Goal %
1. Individual's performance level	3	10	10	333
2. Increased peer pressure—to do a good job	4	7	1	175
3. Employee motivation—to go up and above	2	7	1	350
4. Meaningful performance assessment (good/better/best)	2	8	10	400
5. Incorporating process improvement as a corporate culture	5	10	1	200
6. Achieving bottom-line results	3	8	8	267
7. Perspective on our corporate values	5	8	1	160
8. Increasing our competitive advantage	6	7	7	117
9. Maximizing employee loyalty	5	8	1	160
10. Employee's perceive our compensation benefits to be fair	5	6	1	120
11. Building trust throughout the organization (between levels)	4	6	1	150
12. Relationship building (between levels, across levels)	4	6	1	150
13. Networking within the organization—team-building efforts	3	5	1	167
14. Open and honest coaching and feedback	4	5	1	125

Ranking	Corporate Goal	Business Priority	Improvement Goal %
Not a focal point	1	1	
Nice to have	5	5	205
Gotta have	10	10	

Results Achieved to Date %

Figure 7.6 Training assessment tool—training effectiveness goals.

* Dettmer, William. *The Logical Thinking Process.* Milwaukee, WI: ASQ Press, 2007, pp. 72–88.

goal. It will further be shown in the example of the worksheet that follows the discussion.

Tactical Improvement Area: Individual Performance Levels

The question needs to be asked that, if our intent is to improve the individual performance levels of our human capital assets, how do we go about achieving the increase? The following example suggests that there are three ways to accomplish the goal. First, we need to increase process efficiency. We need to remove nonvalue added activities that are blocking that process efficiency. The second method would be to increase the rate of productivity on the part of the rank and file of the organization. Productivity is based on the amount of product or service that is made or created and sent on to the customer. Productivity declines when we have a large amount of rework to correct errors. The final condition that could lead to higher productivity levels is how well the team works together.

Tactical Improvement Area: Increased Peer Pressure

Peer pressure can be a good thing and it can be a bad thing. In order to achieve the improvement within this tactical area it requires the organization to increase the level of team participation in the organization. We do that by ensuring that everyone is on the same page. You need to identify who is serving as an obstacle to process flow. In that same light, the intent is to get the team together toward a common goal and allow the impact of the team members to work on those who are refusing to come along for the ride.

Tactical Improvement Area: Employee Motivation

This is the 64-million-dollar question for many organizations: How do we motivate others within the organization to perform at a higher level? The answer is based on how motivated the employees are toward their jobs.

Motivation arises out of several directions. The first is pride of ownership. Deming stated that when the employee owns the business, they perform at a higher level. We do not mean financially owning the company. We mean that they take pride in that finished product or service being delivered to the customer. When the human capital assets feel this sense of ownership of the process, it leads to a higher level of employee engagement.

Another aspect of employee motivation is whether the training you are offering is adding to their career portfolio. Is the training adding to the level of skills they have to bring to the table?

The other side of that coin is whether the new skills are leading them to a higher visibility within the organization and opening doors to new opportunities to enhance their careers.

The ultimate benefit of this tactical area is that as you improve it, morale goes up, retention rates improve, and the organization builds a team spirit.

Tactical Improvement Area: Performance Assessment

Do you know who your HIPOS (high potential, high performing) employees are? Do you even know how to assess who they are? In order for the performance assessment tactical area to improve, the organization needs to first know who your HIPOS are and how to assess the level of their performance.

Tactical Improvement Area: Focused Process Improvement

Every organization has processes with hiccups. So the question before you is, how do you minimalize the hiccups? There are three ways to achieve this goal. First, you need to improve the workflow. We do that by aggressively ensuring that the obstacles to process flow are removed from the organization. One way to do that is make sure we are not repeating efforts that would save us time. For example, we don't need HR to do a search for talent and then have the manager repeat the search. Finally, as we discussed in *Achieving HR Excellence through Six Sigma,* you need to review your processes to identify areas where you are not following a standard of work and allowing Muda creep to come into the organization.

Tactical Improvement Area: Bottom Line Results

The way to improve the bottom-line results is relatively simple. You have to take in more revenue and spend less on expenses. In looking at this tactical improvement area, there are a limited number of conditions that must be present to reach the improvement goal in this area. One additional area in this area is to remove the nonvalue added activities that reduce the amount of funds available to the organization.

The final area is that you need to find a way to raise the value of the company both to your employees and the external markets.

Tactical Improvement Area: Competitive Values

Your organization has values. Your human capital assets have values. The questions are 1) are the values in complement to each other and 2) are the accepted corporate values corporate-wide throughout the organization?

You can improve the competitive values area by creating a strong corporate communication program to explain the corporate objectives. Identify what is in the values for the rank and file and why the organization is making changes. The communication program needs to also create a sense of buy-in from all levels of the organization.

Tactical Improvement Area: Competitive Advantage

Why do customers come to your organization? What makes you stand out in the marketplace? These questions are the essence of your competitive advantage. The example of the worksheet suggests that there are several ways to enhance your competitive advantage as follows:

1. The golden grail of HR is to make your organization the employer of choice. It enhances your competitive advantage by attracting the best and the brightest of the minds in the marketplace. Entwined with being the employer of choice is that your retention rates will go up.
2. You provide competitive advantage to the organization by increasing your knowledge of both the market and the processes which serve the customer. This knowledge assists the organization in delivering error-free products and services.
3. You enhance the competitive advantage by encouraging your human capital assets to take risks. You want them to develop new ideas on how to do things your business does best.
4. Another key to competitive advantage is how well you deliver on your promises. Take a look around the marketplace and look at those who have the best brand recognition. They all have in common the level of

quality service they deliver. They all meet the criteria set by the voice of the customer.

5. Finally, the organization must encourage the belief in the system from the nonsales personnel. Those in finance, IT, etc. must also show the same energy demonstrated by the sales staff in business development efforts.

Tactical Improvement Area: Employee Loyalty

Tied to the involvement of your employees within the organization and being the employer of choice is the question of employee loyalty to the organization. Industry has found that if we have engaged employees, we see in turn reduced turnover rates and a lower level of reasons not to report for work.

Tactical Improvement Area: Compensation Benefits

The compensation and benefits area of the tactical improvement areas refers to the level of compensation you are providing to your human capital assets at all levels. As the very basis of the consideration is, are you providing a living wage for your location? When the human capital assets are not treated solely as an expense item, knowledge levels go up along with employee promotion rates.

Tactical Improvement Area: Building Trust

Process improvement is based on everyone doing his or her part to enhance the organization. The result is based on everyone within the organization trusting others. You need to get to the place in your organization where you trust people to provide the correct information when you need it. This same level of trust needs to extend to your customers both internally and externally to the organization.

Tactical Improvement Area: Relationship Building

Interdependent with the area of building trust is taking that trust to the next level and building relationships with all segments of the supply chain. The relationship needs to be established primarily between management and the human capital assets through recognition of the performance levels of the teams and management's willingness to recognize the results of the training programs offered.

Another aspect of this area is that from time to time you will find yourself in a position where you don't directly have the information you need to compile solutions to pressing issues. To operate at your maximum potential, you need to have a wide selection of subject matter experts (SMEs) that you can turn to. You must also trust these SMEs to provide the answers you need.

Tactical Improvement Area: Networking Benefits

Communication within your organization must be a two-way street. The number one way of enhancing these communication efforts is to provide opportunities for human capital assets to network with each other. This includes with subject matter experts but also with informal access to senior management. Management should truly have an open-door policy. The other side of the coin is providing the opportunity for the human capital assets the ability to provide management with direct feedback on how the organization is operating.

Tactical Improvement Area: Follow-Up Coaching

I talked earlier about the need for managers today to be leaders. This evolution included being a coach to the rank and file. This means that managers, in the situation where the education did not take hold, must be willing to coach the human capital assets on how they can achieve the level of performance that the organization needs. This also includes the potential of explaining to an FTE why the best action would be to leave the current job, either for an outside position or another department within the company.

The response to the follow-up coaching is increased employee engagement and a higher level of employee morale.

The TREEAT ask you to make three analysis tasks with the information you now have in your possession. First, you are asked to subjectively answer whether you think the provided training had a positive impact on the corporate improvement area. The question is answered by a simple yes or no.

With that response in hand, on those tactical improvement areas where you responded that it did have an impact, at what point do you expect to see the improvement? You are given three choices—3 months, 6 months, or 1 year. The response is entered by the time.

The third assessment was, in looking at the impact of the training, how effective the training was in meeting the corporate goal. This is different than whether there was a positive impact on the area. This is asking you to determine on a scale of 1–10, with 10 being superior, just what impact the training had.

The results of your assessment are carried over to the later worksheet, as will be discussed in later pages in this guide (Figures 7.7 through 7.9).

Training Attribute Tool					
	Did Training Positively Impact the Corporate Improvement Area?	If Yes---How Long Will It Take to See Tangible Improvements Short Term (≤ 3 Months) Mid Term (≤ 6 Months) Long Term (≤ 12 Months)	How Effective Was the Training in Meeting the Corporate Goal?	Targeted Corporate Improve- ment Percentage (%)	Training Effectiveness Calculation Projected Improvement Results
Attribute	(Yes) or (No)	(3)(6) or (12)	Scale (1–10)		
Performance Levels				333	50
Increased process effciency	No	3	2		
Increased productivity	No	3	2		
Increased team performance	No	3	2		
Increased Peer Pressure				175	87
Increased team participation	No	3	5		
Increased peer pressure	No				
Employee Motivation				350	70
Increased pride of job ownership	Yes	6	5		
Increased employee engagement	Yes	6	5		
Increased career portfolio	Yes				
Increased status and promotability	Yes				
Increased morale	Yes	3	3		
Built team spirit	Yes	3	3		
Performance Assessment				400	(Not effective)
Identified top performers	No				
Assessed employee performance	No		0		

Figure 7.7   Training effectiveness tool—training impact assessment.

				160	(Not effective)
Employee Loyalty					
Reduced turnover	No				
Reduced absenteeism	No				
Compensation Benefits				120	45
Improved knowledge levels	Yes	3	3		
Improved employee promotion rates	No				
Building Trust				150	74
Increased relationship building among coworkers	Yes	6	5		
Maintained customer/end-user relationship	Yes	6	5		
Relationship Building				150	
Increased recognition of improved team performance	No				
Management recognition of effect of the training to the company	No				
Built relationship with subject matter experts	No				
Increased loyalty through career portfolio development	No				
Networking Benefits				167	42
Provided networking opportunities	Yes	3	5		
Provided informal access to senior management	Yes	3	2		
Provided opportunity for FTEs to provide feedback	Yes	3	3		
Follow-up Coaching				125	50
Increased employee engagement	Yes	3	5		
Increased employee morale	Yes	3	3		

Figure 7.8 Training effectiveness tool—training impact assessment page 2.

Training Assessment Tool—ROI Calculations

The third worksheet in the TREEAT is the one that is there because organizations want to keep track of corporate spending. It puts training expenses in financial terms. It is provided because the financial side of your organization wants to know how the expenses you make in training the organization relate to the bottom line and thus the return for your investment.

Training Attribute Tool

Return on investment calculation				Confidence in realizing training impact (%)	75.00%
Training impact:	$37,501.88	<<<<<<<<<<<<<<<<<<<< <<<<<<<<		Total training impact	
Training cost:	$12,275.00			Misc. cost savings	$2.50
Return on investment:	206%			Productivity improvement	$50,000
				Waste elimination	$0.00
				Scrap reduction	$0.00
Training Costs				Quality improvement	$0.00
Instructor	$1,000.00	Trainer			
Materials	$ 275.00	Books/handouts			
Room/support	$ 750.00	Logistics			
Training materials	$ 250.00	Total cost			
Net cost (FTEs)	$10,000.00	FTE total cost			
Total # people being trained	25	# FTEs			
Total training time	16	Hours			
Average cost per FTE	$ 25.00	Per hour			
Total	$12,275.00				

Copyrighted 2009 Daniel Bloom and Associates, Inc. Created by Daniel T. Bloom and William Mazurek
Not for reproduction or distribution without authorization.

Figure 7.9 Training effectiveness tool—ROI calculations.

In completing the worksheet you are operating under the target that the chances of your organization realizing the training impact target is at the 75% level. This means you are reasonably sure that you will at least in part have a positive impact on the organization with the training programs to be provided. The ROI assessment, as other worksheets in the tools, has formulas embedded to carry on further. If you look at the preceding worksheet, you will see certain blocks shaded in a different color. As we change the data in these boxes, it changes the bottom line.

While I believe that the Training Effective Attribute Assessment Tool is a unique evaluation of your training programs, I still am cognizant of the fact that the delivery of training offerings is not free of costs. The third worksheet provides you with the built-in capability to assess your training costs. The process consists of four sets of data.

- Training Costs
  In the training cost dashboard you will find a series of cells highlighted in gray. These are the only fields you need to be concerned with.

Begin by inputting the compensation for the trainer. It should be based on the actual time in the classroom and not the total annual compensation.

■ Material Costs

This entry includes the total costs of the books and materials used in the course of the training.

■ Room/Support Costs

This entry represents the total costs for the room rental and the audiovisual equipment costs.

■ Net Cost (FTEs)

The net cost is calculated by multiplying the number of FTEs being trained by the number of required training hours multiplied by the hourly rate of the FTEs attending the training.

The total of these calculations is entered into the return on investment data block under Training Costs.

The next data fields to be entered involve the impact of the training on your organization. This begins with the assumption that you are offering training with a 75% confidence rate in the ultimate impact on both the participant and the organization.

From here you calculate five specific impact criteria as follows:

1. The first field is a place to enter the amounts of any miscellaneous cost savings.
2. The second field is a calculation of the expected productivity improvement resulting from the training programs you are presenting.
3. One of the outcomes you are looking for is the elimination of nonvalue added activities from the process within the organization. In the third field, you enter the total savings from the elimination of the waste.
4. The fourth field represents the value of the excess material that is eliminated because the training has demonstrated how to save materials.
5. The final field is that of placing a value on the quality improvement resulting from the training.

The total of these impact costs multiplied by the training confidence level is entered into the training impact field within the training

	Jan	Feb	March	April	May	June	July	August	Sept	Oct	Nov	Dec
2009 improvement target	17.11%	34.21%	51.32%	68.43%	85.54%	102.64%	119.75%	136.86%	153.96%	171.07%	188.18%	205.29%
2009 actual improvement	0.00%	15.00%	15.00%	40.00%	40.00%	55.00%	55.00%	55.00%	55.00%	55.00%	55.00%	55.00%

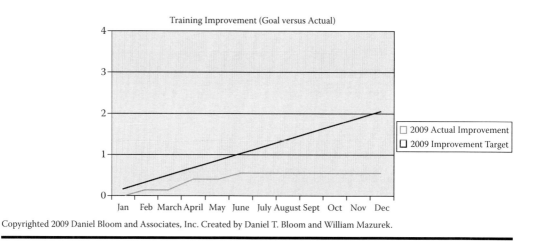

Copyrighted 2009 Daniel Bloom and Associates, Inc. Created by Daniel T. Bloom and William Mazurek.

Figure 7.10   Training effectiveness tool—training analysis.

return on investment dashboard. The dashboard will take the training impact and the training cost and calculate the return on investment (Figure 7.10).

Training Assessment Tool—Training Improvement

In the discussions of Worksheet 1 and 2 in the TREEAT, I stated that the results of your judgment calls would be carried forward for use in a future worksheet. Worksheet 4, shown earlier, is that destination.

In the first worksheet, Training Assessment Tool—Corporate Tactical Improvement areas, you were asked to determine the current state versus the future state of your improvement efforts. You were also asked to determine the business priority of each area for your organization. This created some backdoor data, which is carried to this worksheet.

In the preceding worksheet, you will see two lines of data. The first line represents the anticipated improvement levels by month for a 12-month period. It tells you that based on your answers, this is the expected improvement for the year.

In the second worksheet, the assessment levels you entered for the expected delivery of the impact on training likewise calculates back data for the improvement effort.

If you look at the preceding chart, you will see two lines in the control chart. The first shows the results of the expected improvement by month compared to the actual improvement impact over the same time.

In my earlier example, the control chart shows that in this case the training was not very effective. This provides management with evidence-based information to make actual changes to the process.

Training Assessment Tool—Course Offerings

The final worksheet of the Training Effectiveness Attribute Assessment Tool looks at the course offerings your organization has provided over the period covered by the tool.

Column 1: The worksheet requests your organization to enter the titles of the courses provided. It is recommended that you be specific in entering the titles of the various course offerings that you have provided.

Column 2: The worksheet asks you to provide the location where the training was provided. The information inserted is your choice. You could enter the city and state where the training was given. You could distinguish between those courses that are provided at corporate or in a division or off-site. Equally acceptable would be an entry that describes the location in any manner that fits your organizational needs.

Column 3: It consists of a drop-down menu that asks you for the manner in which the training was delivered. The drop-down menu provides you with five options:

– The first option is that of Instructor Led Training, which in the traditional training programs is with your employees sitting in a classroom with the program being facilitated by a live professional in the role of the instructor.

– The second option is that of Web-Based Training, in which the employee signs into his or her workstation or home computer and initiates the training from a web program located at some other training site. This is different from the next option in that it is all on the World Wide Web.

- The third option is Computer-Based Training in which the employee sits at his or her desk and takes a training program which resides on your organization's internal computer servers.
- The fourth option is Self-Study Training in which the employee is provided a set of materials pertaining to the subject of the training and works their way through the material at their own pace.
- The fifth and final option is that of Blended Training in which the method to convey the information utilizes a combination of the previous methods to deliver the training.

Column 4: It requires you to enter the length of the training. Each and every training option should contain an established expectation of how long your organization expects the employee will need to complete the training, expressed in the number of hours.

Column 5: It asks you to enter the total number of full-time employees that are participating in the training.

Column 6: It takes the data entered into columns 4 and 5 and multiplies the two numbers to arrive at the total instructional hours provided for this particular course offering.

Project Conclusion

This project began seeking an answer to the question whether or not training is first effective and then whether the cost to conduct training was justified. What we discovered was that the majority of organizations on a global level do not make the necessary steps to answer that question. We have proposed a new model for determining the effectiveness of the training efforts, which we believe is easier and more comprehensive then the utilization of the standard evaluation methods such as Kilpatrick or Phillips. Actual use of the model in a real-world environment will be the only way we fully determine whether we are correct in our assumptions.

Case Study 2: Reduction in the Effective Time to Hire

The Organization: A provider of complex and sophisticated electromechanical devices with capabilities that include concept development, industrial design, design and manufacturing engineering, production, distribution, and field service. The primary market classifications served are navigation and exploration, defense and security, medical, and complex systems. Headquartered in Schaumburg, Illinois, the business was founded in 1900 and offers its customers development, design, manufacturing, and distribution capabilities in a highly collaborative environment.

The Problem: At their Brooksville, Florida, location, the organization was witnessing an extended hiring process. The problem was that this process was costing the organization monies in the way of productivity, overtime, management being taken away from the delivery of end products to customers, and costs associated with agency usage.

Figures

7.11 Project charter
7.12 SIPOC
7.13 Fishbone diagram
7.14 Pick chart
7.15 Spartan Electronic pick items
7.16 Detailed activity sheet
7.17 Candidate activity sheet
7.18 Pareto chart
7.19 Sparton Electronics—HR process for filling open positions.

Project Charter Statement

Black/Green Belt Lead	**Quality Manager**	Business Unit / Location	**Brooksville**
Process Owner	**HR Manager**	Project Start Date	**April 15, 2014**
Conf. Call Info		Target Completion Date	**September 30, 2014**
Champion	**Lean Master**		
Estimated Opportunity	**TBD**		

Element	Description	Team Charter
1. Process	Define the process in which opportunity exists.	The recruiting process for salaried positions can yield improved performance in the time to fill and cost per hire metrics.
2. Project Description	Describe the project's purpose and overall objective.	This project seeks to reduce the average time to fill for salaried positions from 111 days to 71 days. This represents a 36% reduction, which brings the Brooksville facility in line with the corporate time to fill plan. In addition, we seek to reduce our cost-per-hire from 13.5% to 9%, representing a 33% improvement also in line with the corporate plan.
3. Project Scope	Define the part of the process that will be investigated. Include both in-and out-of-scope aspects.	In Scope – salary-exempt and non-exempt positions Out of Scope – hourly, temporary, and contract labor positions

Figure 7.11   Sparton Electronics project charter.   *(Continued)*

			Baseline	Entitlement	Goal	
4. Objective	Define the baseline, the theoretical target, and the goal for improvement on the primary metrics: Rolled Throughput Yield, Cost of Poor Quality, and Capacity / Productivity. Metrics *may* be changed to suit your project.	**Time to fill**	111 days	−36%	71 days	
		Cost per hire	13.5%	33%	9%	
5. Opportunity Statement	Summarize the project description and objective in specific terms. Include the Key Process Output Variables, their current baseline, the target level for improvement, and the financial impact.	The opportunity exists to streamline the recruiting process and improve our time-to-fill metric. Our current average time to fill for salaried positions is 111 days. This project seeks to improve that time by 36%, thereby averaging 71 days to fill salaried positions. In addition, we seek to improve the cost-per-hire from 13.5% to 9%. The financial impact will be determined in the measurement phase of the project.				
6. Team Members	Define the team members (number and area represented).	Lorri Kindberg–HR, Alex Guzzetta–Finance, Kathy Ellison–HR, Eduardo Vives—Black Belt/Customer, Paul Ranzo–CI Lean Master, Lisa Haffey–HR.				

Figure 7.11   Sparton Electronics project charter.   (*Continued*)

7. Benefit to External Customers:	Define the final customer, describe their most critical requirements and the benefit they will see from this project.	Our customers will receive improved level of service in quality and response time when we are a fully staffed workforce. The hiring managers will have less downtime of vacated positions, allowing for department responsibilities to maintain performance levels. Peers of the position will have a shortened period of time to carry the extra work load.	
8. Schedule	Key milestones / dates	**Project Start**	4/15/14
	Define scope of project	**"D" Completion**	4/30/14
	Measure current state & metrics	**"M" Completion**	5/23/14
	Analyze data, Gap analysis	**"A" Completion**	6/6/14
	Implement improvements	**"I" Completion** (delay in hiring has pushed back implementation date)	9/15/14
	Control new process & adjust	**"C" Completion**	9/30/14
		Project Completion	9/30/14
		Safety Review	N/A
9. Support Required	Define any exceptional anticipated needs: equipment, hardware, trials, access, travel, training, etc.		

Figure 7.11   Sparton Electronics project charter.   **(Continued)**

Issue	Action	Responsible	Due Date	Comments	Follow-Up	Status
No structure or dedicated resource for recruiting	Develop proactive recruiting strategy/ process	HR Staff	8/8/2014			
Slow response time from managers during resume review	Agreed upon turnaround time during initial kickoff meeting	HR Staff				
Improved skills for sourcing						
Completed Items						
Where are the issues	Define and collect data	HR Staff	5/7/2014			Complete
	Sort data sets	Quality	5/13/14			Complete
	Value stream map	Quality/HR	6/1/2014t	More detail		Complete
	Collect more defined data	HR	6/30/2014			Complete
	Update value stream map	HR	7/8/2014			Complete
	Fishbone diagram	HR	7/8/2014			Complete

Figure 7.11 (*Continued*) **Sparton Electronics project charter.**

SIPOC Diagram

Suppliers	Input	Process	Output	Customers
Hiring manager	Job requisitions	**Start:**	New hire	Corp human capital
Stakeholders	Skills/knowledge	Job posting	Increased organizational skill levels	Managers
Employees	Referrals	Candidate screening	Innovation into the organization through new ideas	Customers
Electronic job boards	Candidates	Interviews		Hiring managers
Recruiters	Job requirements	Background checks	Onboarding	
Social media		Request to extend offer		
Managers		Offer letter		
Professional organizations				
		End:		
		Hiring metrics		
		Reduced time to hire		

Figure 7.12   Sparton Electronics SIPOC diagram.

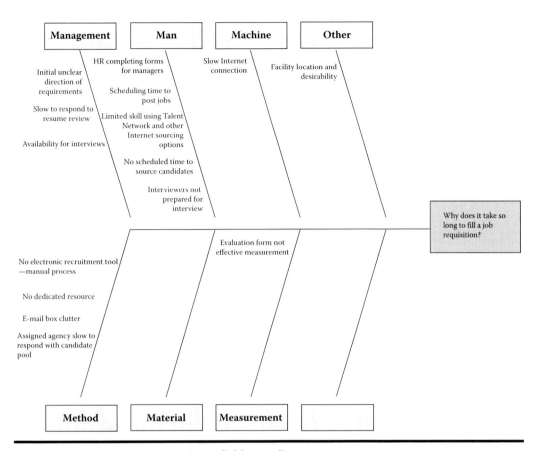

Figure 7.13   Sparton Electronics—fishbone diagram.

	BIG payoff	SMALL payoff
EASY to implement	Work from home on recruiting Set dedicated recruiting time Review agency performance Establish time limit for manager review Establish time limit to send to agency	Separate resumes into their own job folder Meet with Danielle—Tips and Tricks Flag resume submissions mgr Follow-up e-mail to mgr after 48 hours
HARD to implement	Create talent pool of candidates Go to agencies sooner Use Talent Network-Internet connection inhibits Build network Use social media Review outlook capabilities	Referral bonus for external people

Implement Possible

Challenge Skill

Figure 7.14   Sparton Electronics—pick chart.

Improvement items for consideration	Impact	Ease	Cost	Total
Application Wait Process				
Separate resumes into their own job folder	3	1	1	5
Create candidate pool of good applicants	1	4	2	7
Use Talent Network	3	3	1	7
Go to agencies sooner	1	1	5	7
Work from home on recruiting	1	1	1	3
Set dedicated recruiting time	1	1	1	3
Build network	2	5	3	10
Review agency performance	1	3	1	5
Danielle Gusser—tips and tricks	3	1	2	6
Redevelop evaluation form—for future sourcing	3	1	1	5
Use social media	2	4	3	9
Referrals—referral bonus				0
				0
Wait Manager Review				0
Set time limit and date send to manager	1	1	1	3
Follow up e-mail with managers after a day or two	3	2	1	6
Look at outlook capabilities for follow-up or for organizational purposes	4	3	2	9
Give time limit on Sparton sourcing—When do we go to agencies?	1	1	1	3
Flag as URGENT or HIGH IMPORTANCE	3	1	1	5

Figure 7.15   Sparton Electronics—pick improvement items.

Sparton Electronics Detailed Activity Sheet

Action	Time Requirement
Post job internal	10
Post job external	15
Source resumes	2 Each
Forward to Manager for Review	
Prescreen interview	30
Schedule phone interview with manager	2
Schedule on-site interview	10
E-mail candidate confirmation	5
Airline reservations	45
Interview	90
Plant tour	30
Debrief meeting	15

Figure 7.16   Sparton Electronics—hiring detailed activities.   (*Continued*)

Action	Time Requirement
RTEO	5
Contact candidate with offer	15
Prepare offer letter	3
E-mail candidate offer	2
Offer Letter Received	
Schedule drug screen	15
Background check request	10
Pull results	2
Assign ID#/e-mail manager and trainer	1
New hire notification	1
Candidate Starts	
Close job folder	
Record affirmative action data	

Figure 7.16 (*Continued*) Sparton Electronics—hiring detailed activities.

Time Sparton Electronics Candidate Activity Sheet

Candidate	Date/Time to Hiring Manager	Response Received
Candidate 1	6/20/14 11:38 a.m.	6/27/14 6:38 p.m.
Candidate 2	6/23/14 11:46 a.m.	6/27/14 6:38 p.m.
Candidate 3	6/20/14 8:55 a.m.	
Candidate 4	6/18/14 8:38 a.m.	6/27/14 6:38 p.m.
Candidate 5	6/16/14 8:38 a.m.	6/27/14 6:38 p.m.
Candidate 6	6/12/14 5:36 p.m.	6/27/14 6:38 p.m.
Candidate 7	6/12/14 10:39 a.m.	6/27/14 6:38 p.m.

Figure 7.17 Sparton Electronics—candidate activity sheet.

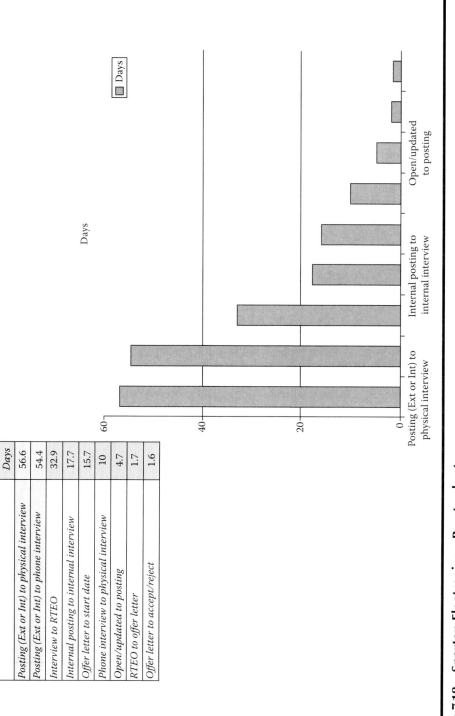

	Days
Posting (Ext or Int) to physical interview	56.6
Posting (Ext or Int) to phone interview	54.4
Interview to RTEO	32.9
Internal posting to internal interview	17.7
Offer letter to start date	15.7
Phone interview to physical interview	10
Open/updated to posting	4.7
RTEO to offer letter	1.7
Offer letter to accept/reject	1.6

Figure 7.18 Sparton Electronics—Pareto chart.

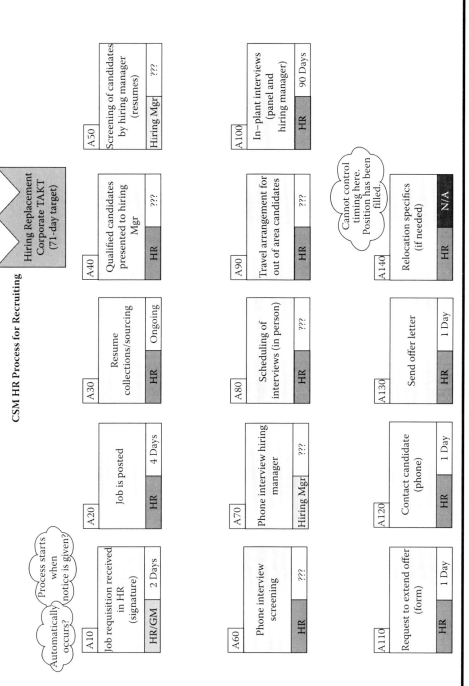

Figure 7.19   Sparton Electronics—HR process for filling open positions.

Project Conclusion

After analyzing the data collected, items from the pick list were implemented and a new process flow chart was developed. During that time, the time-to-fill metric was changed to stop the clock at the signing of the offer letter rather than the actual start date. Taking into consideration the reduced target time to fill, from 71 to 59 days, 59 days became the new goal. To effectively measure their improvement, the team adjusted the original actual time to fill from 111 to 97 days.

In FY2014, the company filled 12 salaried positions with an average time to fill at 97 days (based on the adjusted metric) and an average cost of $5427 per hire. Since implementation of the new process and the writing of this document, the company has filled eight salaried positions. The result is an average time to fill of 35 days and average cost of hire at $1744. Respectively, a 64% improvement in time to fill and a 68% decrease in the average cost per hire.

Case Study 3: Streamline Operations Staffing Process

The Organization: This case study was provided by a manufacturing/development company located in the United States (they did not want their name mentioned); the end product was considered within the industrial sector—total employment at this location, as in the 100–300 total employee classification. The company produces sophisticated electromechanical medical devices with internal capabilities that include design/development of new products and manufacturing distribution, and field service support.

The Problem: Currently, it takes up to 75 days to hire a professional (nonexempt) employee and up to 30 days to hire an hourly employee after the job requisition has been approved. This is causing major irruptions to the various supporting groups within the company as well as eroding customer satisfaction (Figures 7.20 through 7.22).

The Goal: To improve the current hiring process by 50%.

Figures

7.20   Project charter
7.21   Current state map
7.22   Future state map

Kaizen Event #2223 –
Stream Line Operations Staffing Process

To:

Name	Role/Function		Name	Role/Function
Tim McGonnal	Team Leader			
Gozie Mars	HPWT Member			
Thomas Thacker	HPWT Member			
Joann Zimmerman	HPWT Member			
Shannon Ortega	On Call			

From: CI

Subject: **This kaizen will define and stream line current Operations Staffing Process.**

Event scope: **The scopes of the event are current and future state maps including opportunities for improvement Operations Staffing.**

Boundary(s): No Software changes (ATS), no changes to the Excel spreadsheets

This memo is to confirm that the above individuals have been selected to participate in this event. Please ensure that required prep work is completed by the due date and that all participants have adequate coverage to ensure event attendance. We are committed to keeping up with our daily agenda and will adjust working hours according to our progress on a daily basis. As a result, poor event attendance or incomplete prep work can result in event postponement or late working days.

Goals	Deliverables / Metrics

Define and streamline operations staffing processes
 	
Reduce the current staffing process by 50%
	• Future State of
	   - Hiring/Release process (Kelly Services & Permanent)
	   - RRP
	   - Job Postings
	   - Employee Transfer
	   - Shift Change List
	   - Operation Staffing Sheet
	   - Badges/Security

	Monday	Tuesday 9-04-12	Wednesday	Thursday	Friday 09-07-12
Time		10:00am – 4:00pm	As needed	As needed	10:00am – 4:00pm
Activity		BPK			BPK
Location		Bldg 3 Conf. Room 3			Bldg 3 Conf. Room 3
Mgmt Update		TBD			TBD

I am looking forward to working with you. If you have any questions, please feel free to contact me at xxx-xxx-xxxx

Best Regards

CI Team Facilitator

Manager Approval:	

Figure 7.20   Medical device manufacturer—project charter.

TIGER TEAM GOAL

■ To visually map out the current internal hiring process.
■ To develop an improved process map for the internal hiring process that minimizes cycle time, eliminates wastes, and improves operational efficiency through better feedback, communication, and timeliness.

TEAM AGENDA

- Define the current process
- Organizational overview
  - Identify all departments involved
  - Identify functional handoffs
- Process flow analysis
  - Detail each process step
  - Focus on value added, nonvalue added, necessary nonvalue added, and delay operations
- Development new process map and identify open issues / opportunities and roll-out plans

OPPORTUNITIES FOR IMPROVEMENT

1. Job description / posting forms are different. Can we replace with one common job description to do both functions?
   a. FDA requirements
   b. Can it be electronic based
2. Can we standardize the job posting format with the job description format?
3. Posting / internal application forms need to be revised (i.e., to highlight the need for the applicant that he or she must meet the minimal "Basic" requirements for the position or you will not be considered).
4. Posting / internal application—add an note > that job consideration and evaluation will occur only after the close date.
5. What information do we need to capture on the internal application log (do we need gender, race, military history … etc.) and if so, can this information be included on the job application form that is filled out by the candidate?
6. Add the coach's name on the internal application—this will clarify who is responsible for the candidate.
7. Can we implement a preaddressed notification feedback form to indicate to the candidate they are in the pool and being considered … or … they have been rejected?
8. Add a check-box on the application form that the candidate has been notified of job status. No notification > HR will notify before change of status form is put into the system.

9. Can we implement a maximum time (e.g., 3 weeks) an employee can be frozen before he or she is transferred into the new job responsibility?

TEAM ISSUES

1. To develop an electronic database (company-wide) to monitor individual performance issues / write-ups that are below minimal performance.
2. Extended job openings—how do we ensure all employees are notified of their status (being rejected or still be considered) when excessive time is required? What is the poka-yoke solution to ensure feedback to HR and the candidate?
3. Add a signature line on the job posting form.

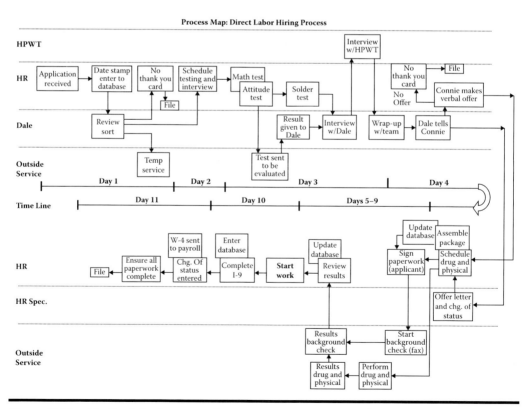

Figure 7.21 Medical device manufacturer—nonexempt employee process map.

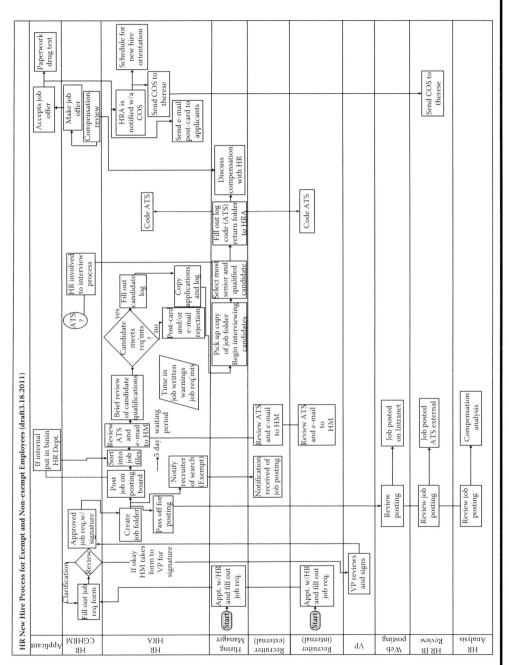

Figure 7.22   Medical device manufacturer—professional employee process map.

ACTION ITEMS

1. Approval of the fixed effective date (2–3 weeks) by senior management.
2. Clean up DOPs and present the process map to HR (week of 5/7)
3. Presentation to a sample of hiring managers—feedback of the steps—postvalidations.
4. Update handbook to reflect changes.
5. Training and roll out to all employees and managers.
6. Revise all forms
   a. Candidate log form
   b. Internal application
   c. Job postings
   d. Create postcard notification form

Project Conclusion

The goal of the event was to establish the current condition ... walk the current process with adequate detail of understanding to frame the current state condition (number of process steps, inputs and outputs, standard work, and instructions and transactions/decision steps along the way).

The Kaizen event was structured using two 4-hour sessions. During the first session of the Kaizen event, the team performed a deep dive into the *current state process flow* for the nonexempt hiring process as well as the hourly hiring process. The current state for each process flow was outlined using "functional swim lanes" (departmental hand-offs between groups) for each stakeholder group alone with responsibilities/activities/transactions and approvals). During this process, we discussed issues (not solutions) with the current flow of information, that is, gaps, bottlenecks, and opportunities for improvement. The following day, we developed the *future state process map* highlighting the improved process flow. The improvement goals were to achieve the 50% reduction in time to hire.

Results—The nonexempt process went from 75 to 19 days (75% improvement) and the hourly process from 30 to 20 days (33% improvement). The team development action items and a detailed implementation plan along with a 90-day control plan to ensure we truly achieved the goal. After 90 days, the nonexempt improvement was 63% and the hourly improvement was 41%. The project was successfully closed out.

Case Study 4: Invoices on Hold

The Organization: This case study was provided by a service provider/ distribution of final products in the United States (they did not want their name mentioned); the end product is various consumer-based e-commerce products—total employment at this location is 350 (three-shift operation) total employees. The company distributes products throughout the United States using US mail, UPS, and FedEx.

The Goal: This Kaizen project was to improve company invoices on hold by 50% (internal error reduction, faster response time).

This company buys and distributes products—when an invoice error occurs it typically results in a supplier late payments—internal/external influences impact the error—this Kaizen event will identify and current errors thus improving supplier satisfaction.

Figures

DMAIC

Project Overview

- Problem Statement: Based on 8 months of data from January 2015, the projected number of invoices that will be put on hold annually due to price, quantity received or quantity ordered discrepancies is approximately 2,916 out of 78,286 (projected) invoices (~3.7%). These "invoices on hold" will require about 500 hours of rework annually.

- Project Scope: Any invoice put on hold for price, quantity received, or quantity ordered holds.

- Primary Metric: The number of invoices put on hold every month for price, quantity received, or quantity ordered issues.

- Project Objective: Reduce the number of invoices put on hold for price, quantity received, or quantity ordered issues by at least 50%.

- Realized Benefits: Reduce labor time and improve the supply chain by avoiding credit holds.

Figure 7.23   Medical device manufacturer—project overview.

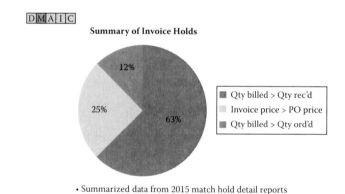

Figure 7.24   Medical device manufacturer—invoice pie chart.

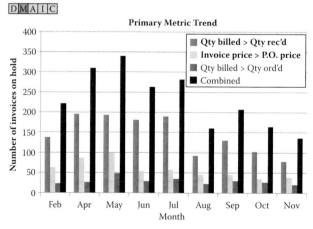

Figure 7.25   Medical device manufacturer—metric trend.

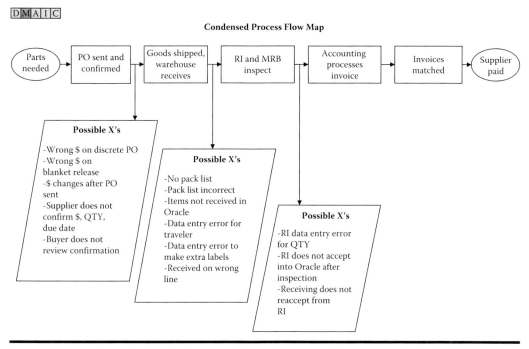

Figure 7.26 Medical device manufacturer—process flow map.

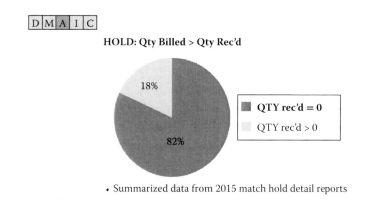

Figure 7.27 Medical device manufacturer—invoice hold.

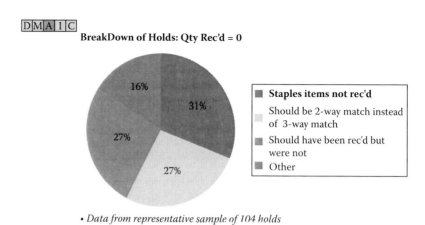

• *Data from representative sample of 104 holds*

Figure 7.28   Medical device manufacturer—invoice hold breakdown.

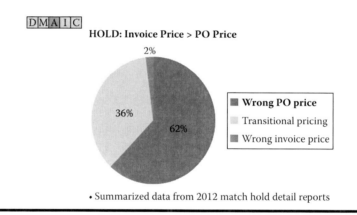

• Summarized data from 2012 match hold detail reports

Figure 7.29   Medical device manufacturer—invoice price versus PO.

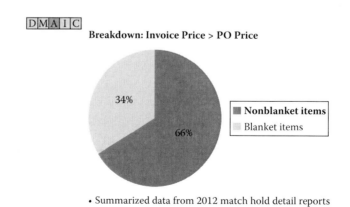

• Summarized data from 2012 match hold detail reports

Figure 7.30   Medical device manufacturer—breakdown invoice versus PO.

Brainstorming on Improvement Option

`D` `M` `A` `I` `C`

Weighted Improvement Matrix		Verified Critical X's (inputs)		Ratings			Invoice Holds	
		Wrong PO Price	Item Not Received in Oracle					
	Significance Rating of Critical X	4	6					
Responsible	Potential Improvements	Impact Rating of Potential Improvement	Impact Rating of Potential Improvement	Impact Rating	Risk Rating	Cost Rating	Overall Rating	Comments
Purchasing	Default suppliers that do not provide physical goods to 2-way matching on POs	7		28	6	7	1176	Will be implemented by 12/14/2015
Purchasing	Add "confirmed" to standard PO headers when confirmed. Run weekly report and follow up on unconfirmed POs	6		24	7	7	1176	Continuous starting 1/21/2015
Purchasing	Retrain CAs and buyers when to use 2-way match		2	12	7	7	588	Will be implemented by 12/14/2015
Receiving	Retrain receiving personnel on which deliveries to receive in Oracle		2	12	7	7	588	Completed
Receiving	Retrain mailroom to check padded envelopes, etc. for POs and receive in Oracle		2	12	7	7	588	Completed
Purchasing	Retrain requisitioners to receive Staples orders as they come in		2	12	7	7	588	Will be implemented by 12/14/2015
Purchasing	Buyers and CAs review match hold report weekly	1	1	10	7	7	490	Continuous starting 1/21/2015

Figure 7.31   Medical device manufacturer—invoice brainstorming.

DMAIC   **Improvement Plan for Qty Rec'd = 0**

Invoice Holds Implementation Plan

DEFAULT SUPPLIER SITE THAT DO NOT PROVIDE PHYSICAL GOODS TO 2-WAY MATCH

Step	Step Description	Individual Responsible	Estimated Comp. Date	Date Completed	Comments
1	Update puchasing supplier add/change form (SI-000-131 2E) so new suppliers are defaulted to the correct matching type on POs	Jo Dextlar			This action item was cancelled
2	Buyers and CAs determine suppliers that never provide physical goods	All buyers and commodity analysts	12/7/2014	Completed (12/6/2014)	This action item was cancelled
3	Change supplier sites to default to 2-way match in Oracle based on lists provide by buyers and CAs	Will Smith	12/14/2014	Completed (12/21/2014)	This action item was cancelled

(a)

DMAIC   **Improvement Plan for Qty Rec'd = 0**

RE-TRAIN RECEIVING PERSONNEL TO OPEN EVERY PACKAGE AND LOOK FOR A P.O. TO BE RECEIVED IN ORACLE

Step	Step Description	Individual Responsible	Estimated Comp. Date	Date Completed	Comments
1	Update Receiving SI	JO CARBON	12/7/2015	Completed (12/5/2014)	DI-000-156 BB
2	RE-TRAIN RECEIVING PERSONNEL TO OPEN EVERY PACKAGE AND LOOK FOR A P.O. TO BE RECEIVED IN ORACLE	JO CARBON	12/7/2015	Completed (12/5/2014)	

(b)

RE-TRAIN MAILROOM PERSONNEL TO OPEN EVERY PACKAGE AND LOOK FOR A P.O. TO BE RECEIVED IN ORACLE

Step	Step Description	Individual Responsible	Estimated Comp. Date	Date Completed	Comments
1	Update Mailroom DI	JO CARBON	12/7/2014	Completed (12/5/2015)	DI-000-152 AB
2	RE-TRAIN MAILROOM PERSONNEL TO OPEN EVERY PACKAGE AND LOOK FOR A P.O. TO BE RECEIVED IN ORACLE	JO CARBON	12/7/2014	Completed (12/5/2015)	

(c)

Figure 7.32 Medical device manufacturer—improvement plan (quantity received).

DMAIC	**Improvement Plan for Wrong PO Price**

ADD "CONFIRMED" TO STANDARD POs HEADERS WHEN CONFIMRED. RUN WEEKLY REPORT AND FOLLOW UP ON UNCONFIRMED POs

Step	Step Description	Individual Responsible	Estimated Comp. Date	Date Completed	Comments
1	Call meeting to discuss new procedure with buyers and CAs	Mike Boyddy	12/14/2014	Completed (12/21/2014)	
2	Create SIs (SI-000-507 Rev AA, DI-000-067 Rev AJ) to specify adding "Confirmed" in discreet PO header	Joe James	2/22/2015		Both SIs submitted and ECO should be completed by 2/26/2013
3	Buyers and CAs individually run weekly report of their unconfirmed POs and follow up with suppliers to confirm	All buyers and commodity analysts	Continuous starting 1/21/2015	Continuous starting 1/21/2015	

BUYERS & CAs REVIEW MATCH HOLD REPORT WEEKLY

Step	Step Description	Individual Responsible	Estimated Comp. Date	Date Completed	Comments
1	Purchasing Admin runs match hold detail report weekly, converts using Monarch, filters results, and sends to buyers/CAs	Ken Jason	Continuous starting 1/21/2015	Continuous starting 1/21/2015	
2	Buyers/CAs resolve match holds	All buyers and commodity analysts	Continuous starting 1/21/2015	Continuous starting 1/21/2015	

Figure 7.33   Medical device manufacturer—improvement plan (wrong price).

Project Conclusion

The goal of the event was to improve supplier customer satisfaction by eliminating invoicing errors (expectation was achieving a 50% or greater improvement).

The first day we reviewed the project scope and goals/boundaries as management defined. We next detailed the current process (purchasing-to-supplier to receiving-to-stocking) via standard mapping techniques (number of process steps and hand-offs, inputs and outputs, standard work, and instructions and transactions/decision steps along the way).

The Kaizen project was structured over several weeks utilizing subject experts focusing on internal as well as external processes. The Kaizen project started by performing a deep dive into the *current state process flow* to better understand all touch labor points and transactions. We also verified computer systems (validation of the data set [price/unit of measure, etc.]). The current state for each process flow was outlined using "functional swim lanes" (departmental hand-offs between internal as well as external groups) for each stakeholder group along with responsibilities/ activities/transactions and approvals. During this process, we brainstormed issues and gaps (causation/root cause of the problem) with the current flow of information to identify bottlenecks/error points and opportunities for improvement. Next, we developed the *future state process map* highlighting the improved process flow along with action items to be resolved. *Variation reduction*—during the measuring system analysis (MSA) phase we confirmed the data collection, conducted a formal MSA and established data collection forms used in the analysis phase—all calculations were reviewed and certified by our internal master black belt. The improvement goal was to achieve the 50% reduction in invoice errors.

Results—The improved process took several months to implement/ resolve. The Black Belt team eliminated 22 hand-offs and reduced invoice errors by 87%. The team development action items and a detailed implementation plan along with a 120-day control plan (measurements) ensured we truly achieved the goal. After 90 days, the improvement was confirmed to be 93%. The project was successfully closed out.

Case Study 5: Documentation Errors

The Organization: This case study was provided by a service organization company located in the United States (they did not want their name mentioned); the end product was considered within the hospital sector Medical Device Manufacturer—total employment at this location is ≥1,000 employees.

The Problem: Currently, the documentation area (close out active work orders) is not following standard work and is not completing all the necessary paperwork transactions necessary to close out a work packet. This is causing excessive rework and 100% inspection to eliminate the problem.

The Goal: To reduce documentation errors by 75%.

Figures

Six Sigma Project Charter

Project Title: Device History Record (DHR) Errors Reduction	Submitted by: Mannie LaNieman
Business Unit/Location: Northeast Operational Unit (NOU)	Date Submitted: 06/11/2014

Problem Statement *(Situation / issue / need for change; opportunity/magnitude; facts/figures/dates):*
From January–March 2015, there were over 105 product Device History Record errors per month, inspected for at 4 points in the process This in volves Quality and Manufacturing resources to resolve these issues, and results in delays in job completions. This project aims to discover and prevent the root cause(s) of these errors.

Linkage to Business *(Identify linkage to business plan / departmental objective/strategic go)*
By improving the quality of sterile DHRs, we are reducing the resources required to resolve errors, preventing delays in job completions, and most importantly, reducing regulatory risk.

Defect fination *(Describe, in measurable terms, what constitutes a defect; this is the basis for the primary metric; no mention of frequency):*
Of the 4 points in the process, only one of them has a metric: NCRs initiated by QM DHR Technicians (level 4). All 4 points in the process inspect for DHR compliance to GMP/QSR and various IP per xxx xxx for, all production departments and QM others TBD.

Primary metric *(Describe project metric and source of data; consistent with problem statement and defect defination; time-series based)*
Primary–monthly number of DHR errors detected at level 3–baseline must be established because errors are currently under–reported.
Consequential Metric–Monthly # of sterile DHR errors detected at level 4 via NCR report.
Sources : High level PFM of DHR review for sterile DHR and NCR M277 query for errors found at QM DHR technician from May 11 through May 12

Present Baseline	Goal/Objective
(Frequency of the problem; indicate average per day, week or month; consistent with Primary Metric) Primary metric - Baseline TBD (greater than 84/mo) Consequential metric - 21 monthly avg. at level 4	*(How much of an improvement does this project aim to make; consistent with Baseline)* 1. Improve primary metric by 75% through prevention or detection earlier in the process. 2. NCR rate at level 4 cannot exceed the baseline.

Project Scope (Where is the focus):
Process bookends: From error generation during product manufacturing through level 4 inspection.
1- Reduce # of DHR errors (new metric) at level 3 by 75% without increasing the number of errors found at level 4.
2 - Since each subsequent level finds such errors. there is a measurment system problem in that they are not consistently detecting these errors. Improve reproducibility betweeen level 2&3 to acceptable level.

Please note: Other activities are done by production DHR reviewer and cannot eliminate all those activities

Impact ($)	Estimated Financial Benefit	Project Benifits	
☐ Low (<$40K) ☒ Medium (<$40 - 100K) ☐ High (>$100K)	*(Rough estimate at the beginning of the project)* *(Describe)* **Total $: 70K/yr FTE hourly + DHR correction + additional resources TBD**	☒ ↓ Defects ☐ ↓ Inventory ☒ ↓ Cycle time ☒ ↑ Service (cust) ☐ ↑ Sales	☒ ↑ Efficiency ☒ ↓ Labour ☐ ↓ Expense ☐ ↓ Capital ☐ ↑ Safety

Figure 7.34 Medical device manufacturer—project charter.

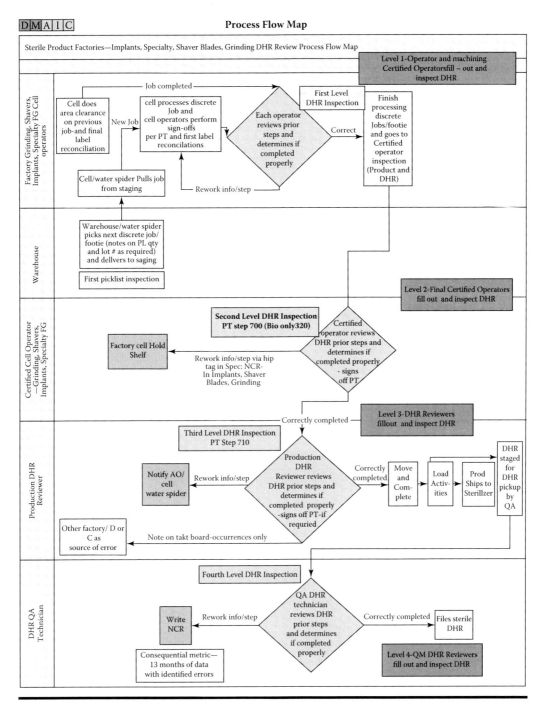

Figure 7.35   Medical device manufacturer—documentation error process map.

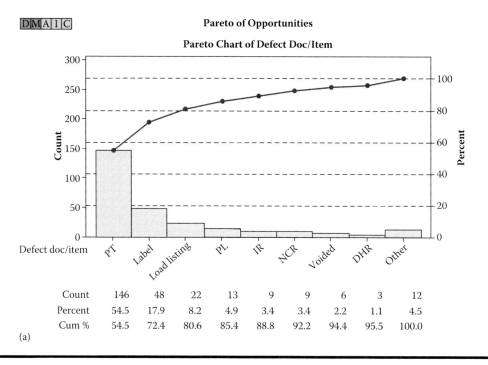

Figure 7.36a   Medical device manufacturer—documentation error Pareto chart of defect doc/item.

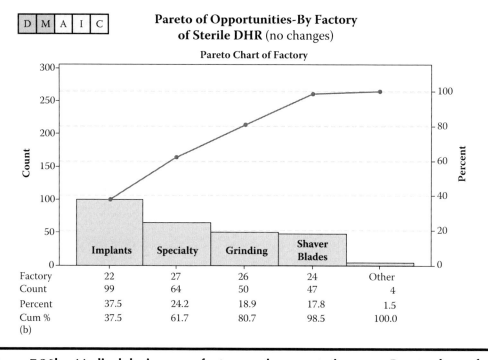

Figure 7.36b   Medical device manufacturer—documentation error Pareto chart of factory.

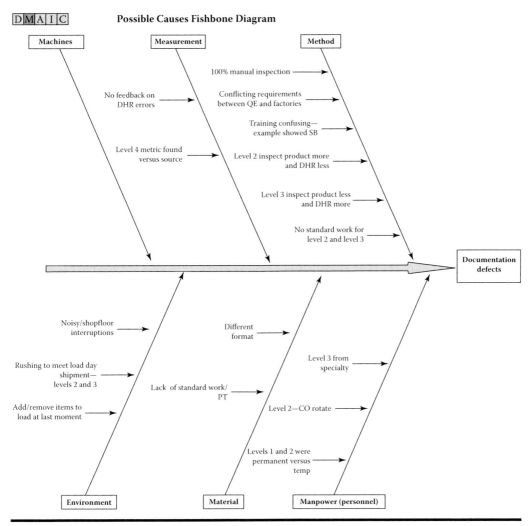

Figure 7.37   Medical device manufacturer—fishbone diagram.

Identification of Critical Xs

D	M	A	I	C

Causes	Critical X	Potential Root Cause	Factory(s)/Level(s) Affected
Environ.	X	Human Error -Rushing -to make load -Load Day (Removal / Add of Job(s) / DHR)	Factory Level 2 & 3
Environ.		Shop floor environ. causes inspection errors	Factory Level 2
Material		PT-lack of Std work for format	Factory Level 2
Material	X	PT-confusing format for count, etc	Factory Level 3
Material	X	PT-no visual triggers for insp.	Factory Level 3
Personnel		Level 3 DHR Reviewers from Specialty	Factory Level 3
Personnel		Level 2 -CO rotate	Factory Level 3
Personnel		Level 1-permanent vs. temp (errors generated)	Factory Level 2 & 3, 4
Method	X	PT in Implants had reversed label requested sequence vs. reconciliation	Factory Level 1, 2, 3, 4, 5, 6, 7
Method	X	100% Manual Inspection	Factory Level 2 & 3
Method	X	Conflicting Requirements between QE and factories for Count on PT	Factory Level 2 & 3
Method	X	Training Confusing -example showed SB factory DHR	Factory Level 1, 2, 3, 4, 5, 6, 7
Method		Level 2 Inspect Product More And DHR Less	Factory Level 1, 2, 3, 4, 5, 6, 7
Method		Level 3 Inspect Product Less And DHR more	Factory Level 1, 2, 3, 4, 5, 6, 7
Method	X	No DHR review Std work for level 3	Factory Level 1, 2, 3, 4, 5, 6, 7
Method	X	No DHR review Std work for level 2	Factory Level 1, 2, 3, 4, 5, 6, 7
Method	X	Error with NCR-level 3 inspection uncertainty.	Factory Level 1, 2, 3, 4, 5, 6, 7
Measurement	X	No Specific Feed Back On DHR Errors	Factory Level 2 & 3
Measurement	X	Level 4 Metric Found vs. Source	Factory Level 1, 2
Measurement	X	In-process audit of DHR review by CO & Level 3 process vs. auditing of insp. results	Factory Level 1

Figure 7.38 Medical device manufacturer—brainstorming improvement opportunities matrix (critical Xs) ID.

DMAIC	Data Collection Plan and Results		
What to Measure (Possible x)	How to Collect Data	Results
Level 3 errors caught via checklist	Special study	DPMO established
NCR data at level 4	Reporting services query	Secondary metric
Results of format changes	Via dates submitted	Improvement

Figure 7.39 Medical device manufacturer—data collection plan.

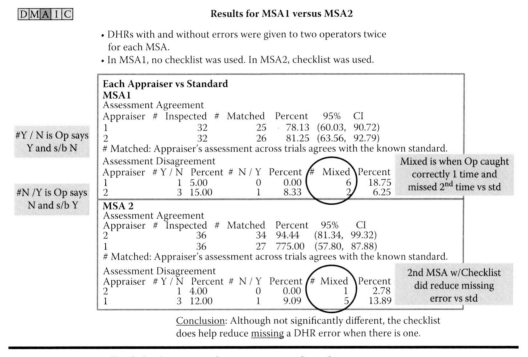

Figure 7.40 Medical device manufacturer—results of MSA1 versus MSA2.

Project Conclusion

The goal of the event was eliminating documentation errors (expectation was achieving a 75% or greater improvement).

Day 1—Reviewed the project scope and goals/boundaries as management defined. We next detailed the current process (purchasing to supplier to receiving to stocking) via standard mapping techniques (number of process steps and hand-offs, inputs and outputs, standard work, and instructions and transactions/decision steps along the way).

Day 2—Kaizen event was structured over 5 days, focusing on internal processes errors. The Kaizen project started by performing a deep dive into the *current state process flow* to better understand all touch labor points and transactions. We also verified standard work (validation of the data set [inputs and outputs]).

Day 3—The current state for each process flow was outlined using "functional swim lanes" (departmental hand-offs between internal as well as external groups) for each stakeholder group along with responsibilities/activities/transactions and approvals. During this process, we brainstormed issues and gaps (causation/root cause of the problem) with the current flow of information to identify bottlenecks/error points and opportunities for improvement. Next, we developed the high-level process map highlighting the improved process flow along with quick-kill action items to be resolved.

Day 4—*Variation reduction*: During the MSA phase, we confirmed the data collection, conducted a formal MSA, and established data collection forms used in the analysis phase—all calculations were reviewed and certified by our internal master black belt.

Day 5—Improvement implementation was to achieve the 75% reduction in documentation errors.

Results—The improved process Kaizen took 5 days to implement/resolve. The Black Belt team eliminated 93% of documentation errors. The team development action items and a detailed implementation plan along with a 30-day control plan (measurements) ensured we truly achieved the goal. Ongoing measurements (real time) were necessary to make sure operator-dependent errors are minimized. After 90 days, the improvement was confirmed to be 91.4%. The project was successfully closed out.

Further Readings

Albeanu, Mircea. *Six Sigma in HR Transformation*. Burlington, VT: Gower Publishing, 2010.

Arthur, Jay. *Free, Perfect and Now*. Denver, CO: Knowledgeware International, 2012.

Ashkenas, Ron, Dave Ulrich, Todd Jick, and Steve Kerr. *The Boundaryless Organization: Breaking the Chains of Organizational Structure*. San Francisco, CA: Jossey-Bass, 2002.

Bassi, Laurie. Applying Six Sigma Techniques to Human Capital Management, July 2006. http://www.dbaiconsulting.com/data/wp/McBassi SixSigmaAndHumanCapital.pdf

Bloom, Daniel T. *Achieving HR Excellence through Six Sigma*. New York: NY: Productivity Press, 2013.

Cox, Allan. *Confessions of a Corporate Headhunter*. New York, NY: Trident Press, 1973.

Deming, W. Edwards. *Out of the Crisis*. Boston, MA: MIT Press, 1982.

DiBernardino, Frank. Human Capital Analytics, the Missing Link: Measuring Financial Returns on the Human Capital Investment. http://www.viennaindex .com/dynamicdata/data/File/ExecutiveBriefing.pdf

Duggan, Kevin. Defining Operational Excellence, 2011. http://www.instituteopex .org/cms/index.php?definition

Fleming, John. *Human Sigma: Managing the Employee-Customer Encounter*. New York, NY: Gallup Press, 2007.

Goldratt, Eliyahu. *The Goal*. 2nd Edition. Croton-on-the-Hudson, NY: North River Press, 1986.

Jekiel, Cheryl. *Lean Human Resources*. New York, NY: CRC Press, 2011.

Lay, Dwane. *Lean HR: Introducing Process Excellence to Your Practice*. St. Louis, MO: Dwane Lay, 2013.

Liker, Jeffrey et al. *The Toyota Way: 14 Management Principles from the World's Greatest Manufacturer*. New York, NY: McGraw-Hill, 2003.

Liker, Jeffrey et al. *The Toyota Way Fieldbook*. New York, NY: McGraw-Hill, 2005.

Liker, Jeffrey et al. *Toyota Talent: Developing Your People the Toyota Way*. New York, NY: McGraw-Hill, 2007.

Liker, Jeffrey et al. *Toyota Culture: The Heart and Soul of the Toyota Way.* New York, NY: McGraw-Hill, 2008.

Liker, Jeffrey et al. *The Toyota Way to Continuous Improvement: Linking Strategy and Operational Excellence to Achieve Superior Performance.* New York, NY: McGraw-Hill, 2011.

Liker, Jeffrey et al. *Toyota Way to Lean Leadership: Achieving and Sustaining Excellence through Leadership Development.* New York, NY: McGraw-Hill, 2011.

Mathis, Robert L. *Human Resource Management.* 12th Edition. Mason, OH: Thomson Publishing, 2008.

Sproull, Bob et al. *The Ultimate Improvement Cycle: Maximizing Profits through the Integration of Lean, Six Sigma, and the Theory of Constraints.* New York, NY: CRC Press, 2009.

Sproull, Bob et al. *Epiphanized: Unifying Theory of Constraints, Lean, and Six Sigma.* Great Barrington, MA: North River Press, 2012.

Tichy, Noel, and Stratford Sherman. *Control Your Destiny or Someone Else Will.* New York, NY: Harper Business, 2005.

Bibliography

Preface
Ulrich, Dave. *Human Resource Champions: The Net Agenda for Adding Value and Delivering Results.* Boston, MA: Harvard Business School Press, 1997.

Chapter 3: Flight to Excellence
Dettmer, William. *The Logical Thinking Process.* Milwaukee, WI: ASQ Press, 2007.

Dictionary.com. http://dictionary.reference.com/browse/enemy?s=t.

Hambleton, Lynne. *Treasure Chest of Six Sigma Growth Methods, Tools and Best Practices.* New York, NY: Prentice Hall, 2008.

McCarty, Tom, Lorraine Daniels, Michael Bremer, and Praveen Gupta. *The Six Sigma Black Belt Handbook.* New York, NY: McGraw Hill, 2005, p. 366.

Chapter 5: Where Oh Where Is the End of this Journey?
Alessandra, Tony, and Michael O'Connor. *The Platinum Rule.* New York, NY: Warner Books, 1996.

Ulrich, Dave, Steve Kerr, and Ron Ashkenas. *GE Workout.* New York, NY: McGraw Hill, 2002.

Index

A

Alumni employees, 16

B

Balanced scorecard, DBAI, 91
Benchmarking, 83
Big data, in HR function, 40
Black Belt Project, 86, 134
Blended Training, 108
Bottom line results, 93, 98–99
Brainstorming improvement opportunities
      matrix (critical X's) ID, 140
Brainstorming, invoice, 131
Building trust, 94, 100

C

Candidate activity sheet, Sparton
      Electronics, 117
Candidates, 16
  sourcing for, 19
Case study
  documentation errors, *see*
      Documentation errors
  effective time reduction to hire, *see*
      Effective time reduction to hire
  invoices on hold, *see* Invoices on hold
  stream line operations staffing process,
      121–126
  training effectiveness, cost justified, *see*
      Training effectiveness, cost justified
Chief Financial Officer (CFO), 16
Chief HR Officer, 17, 19

Clients, 16
Compensation benefits, 94, 100
Competitive advantage, 94, 99–100
Computer-Based Training, 108
Consultants, 17
Corporate culture, 5–6
Corporate governance, 71
Corporate mantra, 69–70
Corporate metrics, DBAI, 92
Corporate tactical improvement areas
  compensation and benefits of, 94, 100
  competitive values and advantage, 99–100
  employee motivation, 97–98
  follow-up coaching, 101–103
  individual performance level, 93, 97
  open and honest coaching, 95
  relationship building, 100–101
  TREEAT task on, 95–96
Corporate values, 94, 99
Critical success factors, goal tree, 47
Critical X's ID, 140
Current employees, 16
Current state process flow
  for documentation error, 142
  for nonexempt hiring process, 126

D

Daniel Bloom & Associates, Inc. (DBAI), 85
  balanced scorecard, 91
  corporate metrics, 92
  fishbone diagram, 90
  project charter, 87–88
  SIPOC diagram, 89–90